A COIN IN A
CAR PARK

A Story of Redemption

Nigel E. Heath

ISBN-13: 9798615947773

Library of Congress Control Number: 2018675309
Printed in the United States of America

CONTENTS

FOREWORD

One of the fastest growing industries of the 21st century has been the emergence of websites enabling us to discover the otherwise hidden lives of our forebears. Thanks to digital technology we can now access records of births, marriages and deaths that relate to relatives we only knew of in a vague way, or not at all. But nothing quite matches the authentic reminiscences of those we have known and loved. In the past we might have learned the stories of our own families by listening as our grandparents reminisced about their own early lives, but in a world where we see older generations only occasionally the passing on of wisdom from one generation to another needs to be a more intentional affair, if it is to happen at all.

This book of personal reminiscences by Nigel Heath attempts to do just that, and more besides, for he not only recounts episodes from his life in a factual way but also reflects on their meaning and purpose. A central theme here is the way the choices we make (or fail to make) can impact not only our own future options but also affect the possibilities of others in our close circles. In the process

of exploring this conviction, Nigel tells a story with
many ups and downs, especially in his early life as
he struggled to find meaning and purpose in what
he was experiencing. The underlying theme will
challenge readers to reflect on their own choices
in life, but the narrative is never dull and includes
moments of amusement and fun as well as crisis and
near disaster. Beginning in Nottingham, the unfold-
ing drama takes us from Wales to Nigeria, with experiences that include bullying in school, wrestling
with snakes, living in hippy communes, finding love
at college in Northumberland, and work as a church
pastor in Scotland. Two things stand out. One is the
importance of community with friends who share
common passions – and the other is the importance
of ensuring that those passions are well chosen so as
to be life-giving rather than the reverse. Ultimately,
this is a story of redemption. You will need to read
it to understand why and how that is so. It is also a
story of divine encounters and meeting God in unexpected places. And of course, it is an unfinished
story, for though Nigel mentions his age more than
once, at only 67 he has another thirteen years to go
before he reaches what the World Health Organiza-
tion now classifies as the beginning of old age. That
must be as much of a challenge to him as he hopes
the story here will be to his readers!

John Drane

PROLOGUE

What do you see when you walk through a shopping mall on a busy Saturday afternoon? More than the shops and cafes are the constant streams of people we weave our way through. Every face is different. With a brief glance we may spot the clues to what events, past or present, have shaped these people to become who they are now. We see the wrinkles, scars, smiles, frowns and hardened determined looks. Some have tattoos. Others walk with a swagger, limp or an elegant gait. People's faces are like book cover illustrations, pointing to what's inside.

Every living soul conceals behind a mask the stories which could form the chapters of a unique and fascinating book. When someone writes a book disclosing their inner secrets, some stories remain untold. Memories of certain events can be too painful to revisit, or too shameful to tell. What might a son, daughter, husband, wife, granddaughter or grandson think if they were to discover what happened to us or learn of the mistakes we made? Where do we draw the line? A book which glosses over, or does not include the painful, shameful stories, with intent to portray the subject a hero can be a shallow and boring read. A book which offers too much disclosure risks for the author leering voyeurism and gossip.

I am often silent. My wife Liz complains that sometimes she would prefer me to be more chatty. We can travel two hundred miles in a car, and I say very little, but my mind is constantly active, recalling memories, making calculations, ruminating and reflecting. I prefer the silence to random radio music.

Behind my own persona is a story I am about to tell it. This book will not be shallow. Some stories will remain untold and will die with me - stories that perhaps I might tell only to a trusted counsellor in a therapeutic relationship. But this book will contain stories that go deep. In doing so, I am taking a risk. I am a person known by some of my readers, shaped by the events I will describe and the choices I have made in response to them. After reading this, you will know better. If you love me, I hope that you will still love me just as much as you do now and think no less of me after you have learned from what I have written here.

Who is this book for? Primarily for my beloved grandchildren Aaron and Sophie, but also for the rest of my family, Liz, David and Charlene, Alastair (Ally) and the wider family including my brothers, nieces, nephews, cousins and in-laws. I be-lieve in the value of recording personal life stories for posterity - for children's children. This book is also for friends, and for enquiring souls to read after I am long gone. I will explain why I chose the title, "A Coin in a Car Park" as the story unfolds.

THE TRIGGER

As we strolled across the wet, grey tarmac of the supermarket car park on that dull winter's morning, there it was, bright round and shiny. I reached down to retrieve that lonely ten pence piece waiting for someone who has no shame to claim it. It was mine. My son Ally mocks me when I pick up small coins. It's a generational thing satirized in an episode of The Simpsons I once saw. Homer bends down and picks up a penny and says, "Ooh, I found a penny. It must be my lucky day".

It seems shameful these days to do what for my generation was the norm - picking up small coins that someone has dropped or throw away. Local schoolchildren descend at lunchtime like a flock of magpies in their black and white uniforms to the food outlets in East Kilbride village. After making a purchase, some of them throw away their small change. Maybe they think it's cool. I imagine it is entertaining for them, watching some senior pick up the coins they have thrown away.

Shopping is something I avoid. I especially dislike manoeuvring trolleys through the aisles of busy supermarkets. Why did I go to the supermarket with Liz that morning? Liz and I had recently returned from Orkney travelling on the Stromness to Scrabster ferry during a storm. The voice over the tannoy system sounded a warning. During the voyage the ship would roll. A strong westerly gale was whistling through the Pentland Firth, causing quite a swell. I looked out of the lounge window and saw gannets speeding alongside the ferry just above the surf. They swooped and dived like fighter jets, dodging the mounting waves and white crests. They were watching for the fish driven to the surface by the vessel as it crashed through the wild sea on its way to the safety of the harbour. It was fantastic to watch.

As predicted, the ferry rolled with sea then sky alternately appearing through the window on the far side of the upper lounge. I lay down on a long seat at the edge of the lounge. For Liz and Ally, the thought of having a cooked breakfast was appealing. They made their way to the dining area and satisfied their appetites. By the time breakfast was over, the rolling of the ferry was severe. Liz struggled to make the short journey from the restaurant to the lounge to join me. An experienced crewman saw she was having difficulties and came to her rescue, steadying and guiding her to a sturdy chair near to me. I was trying not to get seasick and lying down helped.

I was dozing off. The movement of the ferry felt like being rocked to sleep in a mother's arms. But suddenly, the ferry lurched, rolling heavily, as a giant sea swell ploughed into the hull. Bottles scattered and clattered behind the closed shutters of the lounge bar. Luggage slid across the deck, and Liz tumbled from her sturdy armchair and hurtled anatomy over anatomy, crashing to the floor. A small trickle of blood ran from her eyebrow, injured by the frame of her glasses as she fell. But this distracted from the more serious injury. Her thumb no longer pointed to where it should be. A visit to the hospital Accident and Emergency department in East Kilbride at the end of our journey home confirmed our suspicion. Her thumb had become dislocated in the fall. So, with Liz's wrist and arm in a plaster cast, I became her driver and helper that morning for the weekly shop.

A strange providence took me to the car park that day, and finding the coin, lying there on the ground, was the trigger that started me writing this book. I have always had a vivid imagination. During my schooldays, I often opted to let my thoughts drift.

I glazed over whenever teachers droned on about polynomials, auxiliary verbs, antecedents or photosynthesis. I received many a rebuke for "looking out of the window". What do I think about behind the walls of my silent exterior? Here's an example. When I found the coin in the car park that morning, I thought about the butterfly effect - how apparently insignificant events can lead to disproportionately significant outcomes. By "the butterfly effect", I mean the butterfly effect as popularly understood and not in the strictly scientific sense associated with chaos theory. Embracing the popular idea, I imagined what the outcomes might be of finding and picking up this coin. Could this impact events that followed? Could this affect the ultimate course of history, whether personal or global? How could such an impact come about? Could that minor difference of having a little extra money in my pocket make a critical difference to my purchasing power?

Finding the coin led to a change, though not through my purchasing power. This flap of a butterfly's wings got me writing - something I had thought of doing for some considerable time, though I required a trigger to get me started. The coin was that trigger, and now the completed book is in front of you.

Everything you will find in these pages is true as I recall it. Some of it you may find bizarre. Other entries you may find moving or perplexing. What I have written may remind you of small events that have altered the course of your own life. You may reflect more deeply about the choices facing you now and the decisions you must make. Whatever you decide will determine outcomes for you and for others, perhaps for years to come. Have you ever thought about that? Have minor incidents brought about disproportionate outcomes in your life?

   This story illustrates how a small incident can have a considerable impact. It is in part a memoir, but with a difference. It explores the correlation between cause and effect on the present from the past, and the permutations for the future from present events. It seeks to reveal how profound can be the implications of the one factor I have not yet mentioned: Choice.

THE CHOICE

Farewell

Farewell to you, small house upon the hill,
When spring returns I shall no more be there,
Some other hands will tend your garden plot,
Some other laughter linger on the stair,
But in the sunny borders, filled with flowers,
My ghost will sing and murmur with the bees,
And fling the casement windows wide to watch
a Phantom hammock sway beneath the trees.

Soon strangers will reside within your walls,
And gather roses when they are full blown,
Teach them your secrets while they dwell with you,
And all the true contentment I have known.

(Margaret P. Heath (Mum) - 1964)

F or a small boy, it was a routine day. Washed, dressed, breakfast, play with the dog, on with the uniform, brown leather satchel strapped to my back and I was off for the long walk to school. For Dad it would be an extraordinary day with a turn of events that would impact on my life and my future. I was just twelve years old and beginning to adjust to my first year at Margaret Glen Bott Secondary Modern School in Nottingham, 1964. The move to Nottingham from New Brighton on the Wirral took a while to get used to. Although I didn't think about it then, Dad also had his adjustments to make.

Knowing something about Dad helps explain the significance of what took place on this particular day. Born was in Aintree, Liverpool in 1921. By the time he reached his 18th birthday, the outbreak of the Second World War dashed whatever career plans he might have had to be a journalist. Imagine this 18-year-old teenage conscript, now a gunner in the Royal Artillery. What was it like for him to fire rounds from an ack-ack cannon with tracer bullets into the night sky? Did he shoot down invading German aircraft over Liverpool? As a child, I once asked him if he had ever done so. He didn't answer me directly, and I sensed from how he answered that he hadn't. I also sensed that he didn't want to talk about the war.

Through the war, Dad rose rapidly through the ranks to Major Arthur Heath. He had very little to say about the war itself. Occasionally would mention incidents he recalled such as marching into Germany following the Normandy landings. He remembered the smell of death lingering in the air as they marched along the roads.

At the close of the war, the army seconded him to look after displaced persons. Starting at the Rhine, he worked his way upwards to Dortmund where there were barracks full of Russians and Poles. At Dortmund many rackets were being run on the inside. Racketeers locked the elderly in their attics and stole their rations. The insiders were also running a brothel. Dad met regularly with a Russian colonel. The Russian was head of the inside group. He offered Dad a cooked breakfast with large pieces of fatty bacon with a drink of vodka.

Dad in his first army uniform c.1939.

After the war Mum served as a shorthand-typist in the WRNS with the Control Commission in Europe. She travelled from Detmold and on to Minden. In Minden, she visited the Officer's Club with friends. Dad had travelled to Cologne and then on to Minden. He was sitting at the bar in the Officer's Club when the party of Control Commission workers came in, and Dad "saw a pretty girl" among them. Accepting a dare from a friend, he asked her for a dance. She accepted. He then returned to his friends for another drink. Emboldened, he returned to ask what she was doing at the weekend.

Mum joins the WRNS c.1939

Enchantment led to courtship, and in February 1947, they married at Minden and spent their honeymoon in Brussels and Paris. Only a year later they were off to Debundscha in the Cameroons to begin work with the Development Corporation as planters. Dad sailed on the Elders & Fyffes Line freight ship S.S. Tilapa, and Mum followed later on the Reventazone to Victoria (Doula). Mum had already been to sea. She could have avoided conscription because she worked for the United Steel Company in Workington. This was a reserved occupation. However, Mum volunteered to serve in the WRNS. She became a skilled wireless telegraphist working underground in a communications building below the Admiralty in London. During the war in September 1943, she sailed on the SS Orion in a thirteen-ship convoy. During a heavy bombing raid off Crete, they huddled below deck in the ballroom while windows and mirrors were being shattered as the bombs hit their target. The ship, though damaged, could continue, and the crew pressed on out of reach of air attack and landed at Port Said. They learned later that there was a rumour Winston Churchill was on board.

When Mum sailed to Victoria on the banana boat, the Reventazone, it was an entirely different experience to the SS Orion. This was a relaxing fourteen-day voyage. Passengers spent time playing quoits, cards and deck tennis and enjoying the fresh salt sea spray filled air, cool breeze and warm sunshine with the other eleven passengers. Dad had sailed out independently five months earlier in February 1948. At the close of the war it was the Tilapa that brought the very first shipment of bananas into the port of Avonmouth in December 1945. Children had never seen bananas and were instructed not to eat them with the skin on.

Dad had no intention of returning to Liverpool to settle down there. As a child, he witnessed the aftermath of the Great Depression, and sensed the low morale associated with poverty and high unemployment. Dad had a spirit of adventure and wanted to break free from the confines, limited expectations and truncated horizons characteristic of the culture he was leaving behind. His choice to work abroad, along with the important roles he took, undoubtedly shaped his sense of identity and built his self-esteem.

Planting bananas in the Cameroons must have been an interesting start. I guess he got bitten by the African bug. Often, people who go to live abroad for work and fall in love with the country to which they have travelled. Africans also showed great respect to expatriate "masters".

After working in the Cameroons, Dad took a job with the prison service in Nigeria. This was no ordinary job. Dad was the Advisor for Prisons. His work was to teach and train Africans to become prison governors. There was a lot of prestige attached to this position. He found it very rewarding.

So, for more than a decade, Dad became accustomed to being in charge. Workers looked up to him and addressed him as "master" and "sir". They followed his orders. Keep this in mind as I now tell you what happened to Dad on that fateful day in Nottingham and of the determined choice he made in response.

In 1962, when Dad finally returned home from his time in Cameroon and Nigeria, he struggled to find a new direction. What new career could be sufficiently rewarding? Following many years of military service in the Second World War, together with civil service abroad in its aftermath, Dad finally said goodbye to an incredible career. During his career he had was looked up to and admired. Now things were different. It was as though he disappeared, invisible as the person he once was, into a grey and average world, unemployed and with no clear sense of what to do next. He searched long and weary for new openings and finally accepted an offer of work as a representative for the YMCA. This involved uprooting from home in New Brighton to move to Lenton Sands, Nottingham. For Dad, compared to all that had gone before, working as a representative for the YMCA was a lifeless, unrewarding task.

Mum recalled that on the day I am referring to, Dad was visiting a site. There, he was deliberately kept waiting for a long time by a young female employee. Reading between the lines, and knowing Dad, it was a case of male chauvinism meets bold feminism. An unspoken exchange took place of, "*How dare you keep an important man like me waiting*", which was met with "*Who do you think you are? I will make you wait for just as long as I choose until you show me some respect.*" He arrived home that day livid, downcast and resolute, and made a choice. Against all good advice from his well-informed colleagues and the senior YMCA staff who were perhaps wiser, there was no changing his mind. He would leave Nottingham to take up a new appointment with the YMCA at RAF St Athan in South Wales.

Dad found the offer of the job compelling. To Dad, it made perfect sense. Had he not worked with the armed forces before? Did he not have transferable administrative skills? The job was his for the taking. We would soon up-sticks and be on our way. None of us knew then what this meant or what lay ahead of us. As with the metaphor of the butterfly effect, this choice meant that a storm was coming.

What else lay behind this choice to leave? Was it only because a young lady had affronted and humiliated him? Was it simply pride? Or did Dad long to escape from routine, mundane, unfulfilling work and search of something better? I sense the deep impact on Mum in the words of her melancholy poem "Farewell". Mum made a house into a home and was well-settled in Nottingham. She had no desire to move away. The disruption of uprooting again so soon after arriving in Nottingham caused her deep distress. What I would soon discover was how detrimental a move this would prove to be for me and what misery it would cause.

We all know what it is like when we are ambushed by unexpected events. Each time this happens we react and respond. We are like a solitary piece in a row of dominoes stacked on edge next to each other. Fall one way and it will impact on all the rest. Fall the other way and others will topple instead. One bad experience at work when nothing else in life or work seems to go right, triggered Dad's choice to leave. He knew that his choice would impact his family. Perhaps it was a matter of survival. If so, I can understand how his heart would have ruled his head. At any rate, whatever his reasons were, staying put was no longer sustainable. He could have opted to remain. He chose instead to leave.

Though we cannot control the things that happen to us, we get to choose how we act in response. Do we always grow wiser as we grow older? Perhaps not. It was the first century Stoic philosopher Epictetus who concluded, "*What matters is not what happens to us but how we react to what happens.*" I had no control over what would happen next. Loss, loneliness and brutal experiences lay ahead of me as a day pupil within a boarding school for boys in the heart of Glamorganshire. Like an exotic bird escaping from its owner's cage, I would be pecked and picked on. I was about to encounter a new environment in which others would perceive me as different and unwelcome. I was about to discover how a foreigner felt when moving to a strange land.

Dad made a choice over which I had no control. In response to what happened to me, I would soon make choices of my own.

Debundscha House
The road to Debundscha House
Clapping clapping on the back-yard gate
Scouse leather football kicked 'til late
Liver buildings lit by flares
Mersey bombing runs, not scared
To watch the flash and damp the flame
To cross 'la manche' to make his name
A Grocer lad who soon decided
To seek his fate as worlds collided.

As conflict ends so love begins
Of life, and Mum who wins
Bright ruby like crystal with claret and gold
And oysters with romance and a love hard to hold
And American cocktails and smoking 'til three
And parting and meeting and hoping she's free
To the altar together they don't give a care
Dad breathless and dreaming he's walking on air

To the darkest land in search of some light
From the traumas of war and England's new fight
To the black black ebony black
and the colours of earth and splashes of white
To the white white, flashes
of white and the screech of the bush
in the dead of the night
'Will miss take tea'

Or 'G and T'
Before her 'chop' and fireflies flight
late in the tropic, late in the night.

When the special import peels
Its timeless tunes for dancing heels
A whiskey a soda, a spin through the door
Heels clapping clapping on the veranda floor
And now the white ivory yellowed with age
Sits with elders of brass on the African
stage
With patience they've watched it all unfold,
In silence they nod for the story that's told.
(Martin Heath - 2009)

Dad in the Cheetah Enclosure. Probably taken at Enugu Zoo c.1959

THE RESPONSE

From "Ay-up meduk"[1] to "Bore da"[2]
From "Gizzabit"[3] to "Os gwelwch yn dda"[4]
From England and Wales was contrast in culture
What might this mean for my friendships and future?

To be on the outside when others are in
To feel like a stranger with others akin
To be left on your own when others are playing
To be not understood in the things I am saying

Hating the fact that I'm shunned and rejected
Bullied in school I remain unprotected
Educational achievement and mood being affected
Longing to only be loved and accepted

(Nigel E. Heath - December 2018)

T he move to St Athan in South Wales was a disaster. School was worst of all - Cowbridge Grammar School, where I never made a friend. It seems the Welsh pupils hated me from day one for my accent and apparent English nationality. Bullying rose to a new level. I feared and detested every day there. Even the prefects claimed the power of corporal punishment.

One day someone let off a firework inside a desk. The prefects wanted to find out who was responsible. They grabbed me and asked if I knew. I wouldn't say, so they bent me over a desk and struck me repeatedly with a trainer.   Another day, just before gym, I realized that a group was planning to attack me in the changing room. It was as though they took some perverse pleasure in seeing me suffer. Unable to go through with this, the safe option was to walk out of school and head home. I did so and walked the full five miles home along country roads. That was a long way for a boy of my age. Arriving home early was a surprise to my parents. Mum accepted my explanation, but I cannot remember them doing anything about it or taking it up with the school. If they did, they didn't tell me. I carried on at school feeling vulnerable and unsupported.

South Wales had its plus points. My brothers and I learned to cycle. We went egging (looking for bird's eggs). We also went fishing for sea bass in the warm water outlets at Aberthaw Power Station. We fished with rubber sandeels and wax candles that served as a float and weight combined. Shoal bass was plentiful. They put up a fierce fight. On their backs was a formidable, sharp dorsal fin. We had to be careful in case the landed fish flipped over, back arched, and drew blood.

The YMCA centres were at East Camp and West Camp in R.A.F. St. Athan. We had free use of the table football, table tennis, camp cinema and swimming pool. I took delight in overcoming my fears and diving from the top board at the swimming pool. Looking down from so high up was scary. But I learned to get it right after a stinging belly-flop or two.

We had a mouse infestation in the building next door. Mice were a problem but entertaining for us boys. They used to hide in an empty set of drawers in a disused bedroom. My brothers and I tried to guess which draw the mouse was hiding in and then open the draws one by one to see if it was there. If we got it right, it would escape over the back of the drawer and vanish. Once I grabbed an escaping mouse but got a nasty bite. But school was always a dark shadow, constantly in the back of my mind, clouding my every day.

The school staff named us three brothers as Heath Primos, Heath Secundus and Heath Tertius (Latin for Heath first, second and third). Boarding school culture was cold and formal. Richard was the eldest at 15 years of age. Martin was the youngest. He must have just started secondary school at 11. I was the middle one at just 13 years of age. The school was near to the countryside, and the River Thaw ran through fields nearby. We could see small brook trout just under the surface. I recall the mole hills covering almost the entire rugby pitch. The gym teacher used to trap the moles and skin them. He said he was collecting the skins to make a mink jacket, and I partly believed it.

This all-boys boarding school was not the best place for a coming-of-age teenager. It was a typical boy's school with daily break-time competitions to see who could pee the highest up the toilet wall. No wonder it stank like a rancid fishmonger's yard on a hot summer's day. Smoking took place behind the bike sheds (where I started the habit). There was no formal sex education offered at school (or any brave attempts by my parents to educate us in such matters.) I pretended to know everything, but I knew little. I learned gradually through gaining information from stories told by one adolescent to another. These were often a mixture of fact, fiction and half-truths. No-one dared risk revealing their ignorance by asking questions out of fear of certain derision and group humiliation.

I struggled with reading - struggled with schoolwork - just as I struggled to find a friend. Looking back, starting smoking with the others was probably an attempt to find some connectivity with them - somehow to belong. I even tried spitting, but I was hopeless at it and I could never master the art. The headmaster witnessed one of my early attempts and sharply rebuked me. I never tried it again.

School assemblies took place each morning.

These were compulsory religious assemblies in-as-much as there was often a Welsh hymn to sing. My brothers and I became adept at mouthing and mim-icking the words with no knowledge of the language or understanding of what we were singing.

Less than two years later, it was time for us to leave South Wales and move on to Rhyl in North Wales. Dad had accepted another job as manager of a YMCA holiday centre there. We were moving on to a new home for the family and a third second-ary school for me. I was glad to be leaving it all behind. But the pestilential experience of living in South Wales left its legacy, and I have carried the wounds of bitter experience for a lifetime. Years afterwards I made the choice to forgive (forgiveness is a choice after all). Although, when I watch a Five Nations rugby match, it would be difficult for me to do other than support Scotland or England or any other team against Wales. Sadly, I still associate ex-pressions of Welsh nationalistic fervour with being a victim of childhood racism.

These were bitter experiences. I trace the events back to the day when Dad chose to move us from Nottingham. The unstoppable force of a YMCA representative met the immovable object of the stubbornness of a young secretary who deliber-ately kept him waiting. Could it have been differ-ent? What if the young lady who blocked him had been more courteous and kinder instead? What if Dad just put up with it instead? It could have been so different. Altered trajectories lead to different outcomes. But would it have been any better?

The stress on our family was beginning to show. Newly appearing fractures in our relationships would soon grow wider and deeper. The changed seemed to impact me in particular as I developed from childhood to adolescence. Another eventful day was fast approaching. Eventually, matters would come to a head. This time I, not Dad, would face the challenge. In response, my choice would be to leave home with no intention of returning.

BREAKING POINT

MELANCHOLY

I am the jilted lover,
Wounded by the lies of those believed instead of me.
I am the mother in despair,
With child delivered stillborn and never to be.
I am the passenger left in the cold and dark of a lonely
platform for the night;
Who missed the last train carrying the gleeful company
away from sight.
And what I yet shall be I do not know.

I am the son of a father, now wounded in a fight;
Vilified, accused of being wrong when I was right.
Leaving behind the memories of times when life was
fun.
I am the one who was and shall not be, whose childhood
days are gone.
And what I yet shall be I do not know.
Where will I go?

I glimpse the future, grieve the loss,
Resigned to tread the path in company, and yet alone.

(Nigel E. Heath - January 2019)

R hyl was different. A seaside town in North Wales, marketed as "Sunny Rhyl", it nestled on the coastal plain protected within the boundaries of the surrounding hills. I recall the pronunciation of "Sunny Rhyl" in the accents of people from Huddersfield and Barnsley who swarmed to the town each year for their annual summer holiday. Tourists were unaware of just how many locals despised them. Since the local economy depended much upon the tourist industry, contempt remained concealed beneath a polite and superficial welcome.

Ever enterprising, and inspired by the initiative of others, I constructed a cart from an old pram to transport luggage for arriving tourists. During the summer holidays, droves of tourists arrived on the incoming trains, particularly on a Saturday morning. The walk from the railway station to B&B accommodation on the main street was not long. Many of the tourists took lodging there, and the services of a boy with a cart were an attractive option to taking a taxi. It was cheaper for them, and it was good pocket money for us. We busied ourselves under the resentful, disapproving gaze of parked-up taxi drivers who were losing their business to us, and were powerless to do anything about it.

An event that marked my early initiation

into life in Rhyl took place one evening. A gang of youths corralled me into an alley and forced me into a street fight. I had gone out on that dark autumn evening intending to explore the town, but local lads soon spotted me. They probably regarded this limp, naïve young teenager, a stranger in town, as a potential means of entertainment for bored layabouts. The alley led to a small, dimly lit courtyard where I was 'faced off' against a member of the gang with whom I was to fight. He had agreed to fight me on one condition: that somebody remove an empty bottle littering the courtyard (not that I would have used this against him). Whenever others threatened me, I didn't want to fight. Hurting other people didn't appeal to me. In addition, I also feared what someone might do to me if I hurt them. This goes some way to explaining why I was often a target for bullies. And when others picked on me, I would feel fearful, hurt and angry. As I lay on my pillow at night, I would fantasize, imagining myself overpowering the bullies and exacting revenge on those I feared. In my fantasies, I imagined I was stronger than them all. Here I was the hero. Here I thrashed the bullies who'd hurt and frightened me over the years. I could never fully understand why I couldn't carry out the actions of my imagination when confronted by bullies in real life.

My aversion to violence probably went back to having received what I remember to be a rather severe beating, albeit fair and short-lived, from Dad when I was a boy. This punishment was for throwing a stone at my younger brother Martin and injuring him. We were in Africa at the time and had flown out there on the BOAC turbo-prop airliner, the "Whispering Giant". BOAC retired these aircraft in 1962, so I must have been only 7 or 8 years of age, and Martin 18th months younger than me. I can't remember what our argument had been about, but I remember having a foul temper even as a child. I learned my lesson there and then from the punishment I received.

There was a strange anomaly about the way Dad brought us up. He was firm enough with me when I was violent. But then he encouraged us to take up boxing, and to practice against each other. So, I had learned a few skills, and now that others had forced me into a fistfight in this courtyard, I could at least defend myself. This confrontation was no worse than I had faced before. Again, the greater thing I feared beyond being hurt was causing an injury to the other guy. I pulled my punches or deliberately missed my target. And so the fight began.

Looking back, the exchanges were rather tame. I used my boxing skills, mostly in defence. A few days later I discovered that the guy who had challenged me attended the same secondary school I was going to. To my delight, I also learned that I had given him a black eye. I felt rather proud and hoped I might have secured a reputation that would make my future safer.

I still loathed school, not only because of

the bullies, but because I struggled with my work. Teachers didn't help. Taking it in turns to read out loud was an ordeal. I recall one occasion when the sentence I was to read was about the people "*warming their hands by the brazier*". You got it. The only brazier I knew of was an item of ladies' underwear. I read the sentence out loud. "*Brazier Heath, brazier!*" came the corrective from the stern English teacher to cackles of laughter from the class.

My O grades first time around were poor. The head teacher gave me the opportunity to repeat the year, and I did. The outcome was marginally better at the end of this. However, the guidance staff let me down gently, steering me away from any expectation I had of staying on to do advanced level studies. They were not offering me this option. Now, I had to consider options. What was I leaving school to do? What work should I take, or career path should I follow?

Homework and schoolwork were often marked, with lines of red ink and the regular comment, "*Careless work*". This comment always shut me down. I did care. What they meant was I should take greater care when completing it. Had I understood this, I might well have made a greater effort. Stated positively, "*Take more care*" would have been more constructive. I imagine most of us respond better to the carrot than the stick.

In the autumn of 1968, I began an apprenticeship at Hawker Siddeley in Broughton near Chester. It was an early start at about 6.30 in the morning taking the works coach. I bought a newspaper, but being tired, I kept rubbing my face with my hands. No-one cared to tell me I had fingered smudges of newsprint all over my face. I only discovered this when I went to the toilet during the first tea break.

The apprentice warehouse was full of rows upon rows of noisy lathes and milling machines. The air was filled with the unmistakable smell of white coolant which seeped into our standard issue navy blue overalls. Making machine parts on the lathe was enjoyable enough. But I disliked the hang-dog atmosphere, the cursing, coarseness, the Page 3 semi-clad pictures taped to the canteen wall, the tea-stained enamel mugs. In addition, the day-re-lease college studies were more than I could cope with. Maths was never my strongest subject. I was drowning and not putting the work in. Exams were fast approaching. My stomach was in knots every time I thought of sitting at a desk over a blank sheet with an equally blank mind.

The stress got to me. I stopped going in to work at Hawker Siddeley without telling my par-ents. Dad was busy and set out each morning for his work at 6.30 a.m., returning late at night. The only times I heard from him were when he thought I needed correction. Other work was readily avail-able at the local amusement arcade. It was tempor-ary, cash-in-hand work, and my parents were none the wiser that I was going there instead.

One day I returned home to discover that someone from Hawker Siddeley had called into the house to ask why I hadn't been at work. He had come and gone, and Dad was waiting for me, simmering with rage. He'd found out from someone else what he didn't know about his own son. It was the closest he ever came to being violent with me, pushing and shoving me against the wall. This hurt me deeply. Worse was to come.

I was now seventeen and the hormones of adolescence were in full flow. I had developed a total crush on a certain young lady who had taken summer work at the YMCA holiday centre where Dad was the manager. It was unrequited love. I learned the hard way. This was the first time I plucked up courage to make a move. The response I dreaded followed. Carol voiced the dismissive words I had braced myself for, "*I love you as a brother*". Wounded, I learned how every young guy feels when, infatuated by some pretty lady, he finds out the hard way that she doesn't feel the same way about him. She tells him so, and he now has to live with the embarrassment and gossip.

Carol was the first person to introduce me to dope[5]. I knew enough about the danger of opioids to avoid them. Cannabis was not an opioid. I found Carol's description of the recreational effects of smoking a joint[6] compelling. She told me where I could score[7] some dope in the town. Curiosity got the better of me and I began to smoke it. One day I learned that Carol's friend, who also worked at the YMCA, had started using class A drugs. Concerned for her safety, I wondered what I should do. I confided in another young staff member. We agreed that it might be best to inform the local G.P. who was responsible for the medical care of the staff at the YM. I thought that would settle it, but trouble was coming.

It happened late on one dark evening. I was heading out as Dad was returning home. It was obvious he had been drinking. Something had got into him that night. We met on the narrow, dimly lit pathway next to the house. It was then that he launched into a stream of criticism. He disappointed he was in me. My memories of the conversation are vivid. He accused me of being irresponsible. I countered, so he asked me to give him just one example of when I had taken responsibility for anything. At this point I told him what I had kept secret until now: my concern about Carol's friend and her opioid abuse. In my mind, I had done the responsible thing. This should win him over. He asked the question. I gave the answer. I told him what I had said and done in reporting my concerns for her well-being. But instead of acknowledging this, Dad went ballistic. In an outpouring of pure rage, he launched into a relentless verbal attack: "*I wondered who it was who had been going around spreading rumours...*". The words faded into background noise. I remember nothing else he said, but I remember everything I felt. That evening was one of my worst in living memory. I walked off into the night with tears streaming down my face and headed for the beach. Blinded by tears and rage, I stepped into the traffic causing a driver to make an emergency stop. I glanced at the driver and saw his expression turn from shock and anger to bewilderment and sympathy. He could see I was in a state. I went over and over Dad's words in my head. Dad had rubbished the one thing I was proud of. He left me with nothing. Charmed by the lies and pretence of young, pretty ladies, he had believed their denials and was out to get their accuser. That accuser was me. That night I recalled something else Dad had said to me on more than one occasion: "*While you are under my roof, you do as I say*". Deeply wounded, that very night that I decided to leave home at the first available opportunity.

The experience redefined my relationship with Dad from that day on. A chance encounter by the house and the exchanges that followed sowed the seeds of bitterness. The roots of bitterness continued to grow. I would, in just a few years' time, seek to root these out with limited success. Choosing to forgive is one thing, but when feelings die, it is difficult to bring them back to life again.

Secret planning and preparation followed, and just a few weeks later my elder brother Richard and I were off to Europe for a holiday. Richard was riding his Royal Enfield Interceptor 750cc with a V twin engine, and I was the pillion passenger. We rode south through France and down into Italy, making our return journey north, reaching Belgium and Holland. On our return I packed my bags, left without saying goodbye and went to live in Birmingham where Richard was studying at University. It didn't occur to me at the time what pain this must have caused my mother. Only when I was much older did I realize this. I had stepped into freedom, but still didn't know who I was, where I was going or what to do with my life. The hippie years were about to begin.

Nigel (left) with Richard to the right in Liege, Belgium 1969

THE HIPPIE YEARS

Distant dream
Dawning possibility
Developing hope
Decision made
Day dawns
Loyal friendships
Love and laughter
Live the dream
Lose the plot
Leave it all behind
Find the plot
Forge the dream
Love and laughter
Loyal friendships
New Day dawns
Decisions made
Developing hope
Dawning possibilities
Dreams fulfilled   (Nigel E. Heath - January 2019)

The incident with Dad and the choice I made in response set the course of my life on an entirely new trajectory. I was neither wise nor mature enough to do other than walk away. The thought of living free from the restraints associated with living under Dad's roof was very appealing. I have seen a pattern here. Major turning points in life, both for Dad and for me, were in times of crisis. When this happened, both of us chose to leave one set of circumstances in search of something better. This inevitably meant moving to a new location.

I left Rhyl knowing what I wanted to leave behind, but not knowing what this new road would lead to. I had limited life experience to equip me to handle the new circumstances I was about to en-counter. I arrived in Birmingham in the autumn of 1970 at eighteen years of age. Mature chestnut trees lined the boulevard pavements. Deep layers of crisp, brown leaves swept from the branches of the trees by the autumn winds, gathered into pools along the pavements. The leaves rustled with every step. I ploughed through them, sometimes hand-in-hand with Sue, my new girlfriend and stray dog Scruffy who, one day, had adopted me and tagged along behind ever since.

The musical lilt of the Birmingham accent was different to the hybrid accent of Mancunian,

Liverpudlian Welsh spoken by the people in Rhyl. I settled into a rented flat at 72 Sandford Road, Moseley Village, unfurnished with no carpets and no bed, just a mattress on the floor. I was free. There were plenty of employment options. My first job was as a computer coder, then later with Patrick Motors in Solihull where I learned to clean and polish the paintwork and interior of second-hand cars.

I looked for company at what became my regular drinking den, the Bull's Head in Moseley. There I met with and made new friends who embraced the hippie ideals and culture I was becoming increasingly attracted to. I fitted in well with my long hair, tie-dyed tee-shirt, flared jeans and trademark sandals worn with bare feet.

The Bull's Head was an easy place to score - not referring to women, but to drugs of various kinds, especially cannabis and LSD. There was a whole new language to learn and culture to adopt. My vocabulary grew to include the names of various substances, practices and attitudes: speed, mandies, dropping acid, smoking s**t, joints, spliffs, uppers, downers, horse and turning people on to acid.[8] People were "plastic" and the police were "pigs", okay was "cool", the common greeting was "Peace man, peace" and the gratuitous common cliché, "Far out, man!"

From time to time, the "pigs" turned up in casual dress for a drink at the Bulls Head, seeking to monitor activity. They thought we wouldn't notice them. They were hopeless as spies, not realizing how incongruous they looked - their presence and body language fooling no-one, despite their attempts to blend in. They reminded me of cartoons I had seen of the wolf dressed up as grandmama, complete with frilly bonnet in the story of Little Red Riding Hood. I don't recall them ever making an arrest.

It was easy for people to get into drug dealing. Smokers of dope with a regular habit soon realized that instead of forking out good money for a quid stick[9] it was possible to do it for free. The way to do it was to buy a "weight"[10] for £12 from a dealer, then cut it into sixteen strips, wrap twelve of them in tinfoil, sell them and smoke the rest. Drugs and cash changed hands regularly at the Bull's Head, right under the noses of the pigs who missed it all. This was small scale dealing. Notorious dealers we knew of went abroad to source their stock. Two of them returned from a trip abroad, bringing back a large consignment of Nepalese cannabis resin concealed in the tyres of a brand-new Range Rover Mk 1.

I was fast becoming a hippie. I gathered with friends in their place or mine to listen to music. We played Pink Floyd, Crosby Stills and Nash, Mamas and Papas, Jefferson Airplane, Cream, the Doors, Santana, Cat Stevens and Jimi Hendrix. Purple Haze and All Along the Watchtower sounded loudly. The air was heavy with the sweet incense of smouldering dope, oozing from joints or chillums constantly passed from person to person. The walls and floors vibrated with the pulse of the sound of the music played on full volume. Each of us drew the smoke deeply and directly into our lungs from cupped, closed hands. Cupping hands created a cavity. We tucked the joint neatly between our fingers. Goodness knows what harm we were doing to our lungs, but this was the way to get the greatest intake and strongest hit.

It became more than a habit for me; it became a way of life. Not a day went by without being stoned from morning till night. The hallucinogenic LSD was my other drug of choice. I knew to stay well away from physically addictive drugs like heroin, but lost count of the number of times I dropped acid. When we used it, it took about twenty minutes for the effects to hit. The hallucinations were not seeing things that were not there. Everything appeared to be constantly swirling. Persistence of vision left tracers behind every object that moved rapidly. LSD heightened my sense of perception, distorting my comprehension of ordinary events. I began to interpret ordinary experiences in new ways. A bacon sandwich became sliced pig inside flat, baked wheat, dripping with mingling butter and fat - enough to turn anyone on a trip into a vegetarian.

There was always danger in taking acid. I am not sure if it was true, but we heard horror stories of people 'tripping' who, believing they could fly, threw themselves out of windows. It sounded like propaganda to us - some fictitious story spread around to deter people from going down the road that we had taken. Occasionally people would have a 'bad trip'. I heard one guy go through the terrors and torment of this while high on acid. On another occasion a Scottish friend who was staying over at my place dropped acid and had a bad trip. For some unexplained reason he defecated in the empty bath and didn't clean it up. It puzzled me why, but he was too embarrassed to admit it. Who else could it have been? He didn't tell me what went through his mind that night.

I experienced a bad trip once when I took mescaline. On the trip I became tormented by wave upon wave of the essence of inescapable, over-whelming terror, the likes of which I had never ex-perienced. Beads of perspiration pooled all over my ashen face. I had no control over it and couldn't make it stop. I ran around the block, hoping it would go away. It made no difference. I ate almost half a bag of sugar because I'd been told that sugar took you down from a high. It made no difference - not even a placebo effect.

The trip finally subsided. What I didn't ex-pect was what happened the following day. I had taken no drugs, but the symptoms returned with flashbacks. I became overwhelmed once more; plunged into exactly the same inescapable essence of terror I had experienced on mescaline the day before. I was desperate. I prayed, bargaining with God that if he would take the horrors away, I would never take drugs again. In desperation, I finally went to the GP. He prescribed Librium, a medication to relieve the symptoms, and the flashbacks stopped. Now that I felt safe again, true to form, I eventually reneged on my bargain with God and carried on as I had before.

They say that if America sneezes Britain catches a cold. 1960s hippie values, lifestyle and ideology had drifted over from the States and inculturated the lives of people in the towns and cities of the U.K. I met hippies from all over - Scots John, and Frank and Dee from England and many others. Being young and naïve, I thought hippies as a movement could change the world. How could we do it? Get as many people as possible to take acid. They would see the world as we do. They would see how much of this world is plastic.[11] Opt out of society. Ban the bomb. Promote the idea that everything should be free. Love should be free. Live a simple lifestyle. Live off the land. These were the ideals we pursued. It was with this in mind that a group of us got together and agreed to move from Birmingham to Hereford to live the dream. Opting out of society, however, was neither workable nor realistic. I got a job in Hereford working at Bulmer's cider factory on the Strongbow Keg line, filling aluminium barrels for distribution. Employees placed a bucket beside the hose and constantly filled it with cider for anyone who fancied a drink. I frequently imbibed.

Soon, all seven of us who had formed a mini commune were on the move again. What triggered

the move from Hereford to Harold Road in Walthamstow London, I cannot remember, but I was
happy to go with the others. I had found friendship and the sense of belonging I looked for. Where
else would I go? What else would I do? With them,
I experienced love and affection even when I was
stupid. On one occasion when I had no money for
dope, I bought some cough medicine and took a
very high dose to induce a high. It made me so sick
that I lay on my bed writhing in considerable dis-
comfort. Instead of being told I was an idiot (which
I knew I was) I experienced tangible love, affection,
care and concern from Sue who I was with. I am
still reminded of this when I hear the line in Robbie
Williams song Angels. It's the words, "*And through
it all she offers me protection lot of love and affection
whether I'm right or wrong*". It's the right or wrong
bit that counts - being loved even when we get it
wrong - especially when we get it wrong. This is the
kind affection that blessed souls experience from
a caring grandmother, devoted Mum, or good true
friend.

And so, we were off again to London; a brick
and tarmac and concrete jungle compared to the
countryside surrounding Hereford. In London we
guys began work at a dynamo and starter motor
reconditioning unit. The workshop on the first
floor of a semi-derelict building in Hackney Downs.
There was a skilled young Turkish guy operating
the lathe and a few Jamaicans who, like us, smoked
ganja. They shared their dope with us. I loved

the way the Jamaicans spoke with one another but could never understand why they addressed one another as "bloodclaat"[12].

During one shift at the workshop (I was at home, but the others were there) the workshop floor suddenly gave way under the weight of all the metal. Everything collapsed to the floor below: the lathe, the workers, the dynamos and starter motors stacked high on metal shelves along the walls, all tumbling in. Frank was one of our guys on shift that night, and he came home to tell us the news. Remarkably, he was uninjured, as were all the others. He said, "*If I didn't believe in a God before, I do now.*" This accident meant employment ceased at Hackney Downs. I had to find another job and started at the Leytonstone Wastepaper Company recycling cardboard boxes.

Life's twists and turns can spring surprises. We don't know what's around the corner. Sometimes circumstances change quickly. I didn't appreciate that within a short time a dramatic turn of events would result in my moving on from London, leaving my friends behind. I was unaware that my mental health had deteriorated, and oblivious to how bad this would eventually become. It is difficult for me to trace whether there was one particular cause or a combination of several contributory factors. Taking an extraordinarily high dose of acid didn't help. This took place in Hyde Park, London. The acid, Californian Sunshine by name, was handed to me on a dab of blotting paper from liquid in a bottle. It was the most powerful trip I ever had. The prolonged use of cannabis may also have been a factor. Eventually, my mind became deeply disturbed and I would start having psychotic episodes. This was yet to come.

At Leytonstone Wastepaper Company there was an enthusiastic Jamaican Christian working with us. He was part-time pastor at a neighbourhood church. One day at work, compelled to seize the moment, he told his story to me and to another worker with me. He spoke of his conversion to Christ, and of his plans to return to Jamaica to work with a church there. He was very excited about this. The other guy working with me sneered and glanced at me to get me to collude, but I listened with respect. While he was speaking to us, "Amazing Grace" came on the radio. The Jamaican guy became even more animated. For him, this was a sign from God. He said God put it on the radio just then to back up his message to us. Maybe he said a prayer for me. I think he probably did. If he did, he would have never known how fully God would answer his prayers. His story stirred something in me like the stirring of the waters of a still pond. Had he not chosen that moment to evangelize, perhaps the developments soon to follow may never have taken place. The course of my life was about to change.

❖ ❖ ❖

WINDSOR PARK

You were the father but now you're the son
Now understood for the things you have done
You were resented but now you're forgiven
I understand better what caused your derision

You were the victim as well as the cause
You had your good points as well as your flaws
You had your challenges, I had my fears
You had your own troubles and shed your own tears

(Nigel E. Heath - January 2019)

I t is strange how parents who are long gone, live on within our minds as though they were still with us. Researching, reflecting and writing about Dad has resulted in an unexpected outcome for me. I feel my attitude towards him is now kinder and more understanding than perhaps it ever was. If I were to be honest, in retrospect I had always felt some residual resentment towards Dad for not being the father I needed. I had forgiven him, but the forgiveness that I could offer was a cerebral forgiveness; a ticking of the box "forgiven," a compartmentalized act, a choice, borne out of a sense of obligation to God. That act, however, didn't fully address or change my feelings of resentment altogether. Now, at nearly 67 years of age, I am writing about a father who was just 43 years old when he returned from Africa. This man was desperately trying to reinvent himself. He was trying to find his vocation and was looking for direction. Now that I am older than Dad was then, I feel like a father thinking about a son. If he were my son, I would be far more sympathetic. I see him in a very different light. I don't think he found what he was looking for. He settled for the best job he could come up with. He was on a journey with no clear destination, not knowing how things would turn out.

Dad made mistakes. I too made mistakes and I'm haunted by them. Regularly memories of many a faux pas rudely ambush me. These intruders disturb my peace of mind and make me restless and often overcome with a sense of guilt or regret. Random interventions can trigger painful memories of stupid things I have said or done. There is no escaping this. I could be sitting in a chair, watching TV, out at the supermarket or driving the car when tormenting thoughts return. My "tell" is a slight shake of my head from side to side in response to feelings of deep anxiety. I wish I wish I could turn the clock back on my life and do a retake for each regrettable action or inaction. I have altered the course of other people's lives by my words and deeds. I hope and pray for the people I may have hurt, that they may find consolation and recovery. Rightly, they may feel the same resentment towards me that I once felt towards my father. I also hope that I may have been of help to many others. Maybe I have altered the trajectory of the lives for immense good through simple, positive interventions, just as the Jamaican worker at Leytonstone Wastepaper Company did for me.

Back at Harold Road in Walthamstow, London, gathered with my hippie commune friends, I was becoming increasingly unsettled. I lived in a perpetual mental fog. The daily norm was a dope-induced, muted consciousness after smoking the first joint early in the day. It was now August 1972 and two full years had passed since I had left home. News came to us of a free rock festival being organized by Bill "Ubi" Dwyer to take place in Windsor Park. Ubi Dwyer was apparently an employee in Her Majesty's Stationary Office. But his employers appear to have been unaware that he had been imprisoned by the Australian authorities in 1968 and deported to Ireland a year later. Scheduled to play were the bands Hawkwind, Pink Fairies and Brinsley Schwarz. I had a strong intuitive feeling that I should be there and was determined to go.

Arriving at Windsor Park, I joined in with the gathering crowds. Little forethought or planning had gone into arrangements for the event. There was no stage, fence, gates, stewards or toilets. The bands were playing on a low platform constructed from timber. Someone had supplied a petrol generator to provide electric power. The generator hummed and fumed in the background and kept breaking down. Every time it broke down, the sound immediately faded, and the band had to stop playing mid-tune.

Windsor Park Pop Festival looked and felt like a small-scale Glastonbury event. There were about 700 people in attendance. I attended Glastonbury in 1971 with a line-up including Hawkwind, Melanie, David Bowie, Joan Baez and Fairport Convention. The Windsor Park event was much lower key. The Crown Estates Commission had not granted permission for the event, but the organizers went ahead anyway.

An eclectic mix of squatters, commune dwellers, anti-monarchists, hippies and rebels of various kinds gathered in growing numbers. They were among those who were chasing the illusory ideals of peace and harmony in a deconstructed world epitomized by John Lennon's songs "*All You Need Is Love*" and "*Give Peace a Chance*". Also present was what I would describe as a 'spooky' group of people who were possibly Satanists, probably involved in witchcraft and the occult. They had billed the festival as the rent-strike concert. This resonated with anti-government angst towards the Tories, who had recently increased council tenant rents to bolster funds for the depleted coffers of the exchequer. They deliberately arranged for the event to take place in the grounds of Windsor Park, the back garden of Royalty, almost as a statement. The 'Brotherhood' Commune of Holland Road turned up, as did the 'Divine Light Mission' and the 'Children of God' both intent on proselytizing amongst the hippies for their cause. People camped out in tents and tepees, most of them stoned on dope or acid. Sanitary conditions were awful. For toilets, people headed over to a small wood on the hillside nearby.

The Children of God were a notorious sect founded by David Berg, who typecast himself as Moses and communicated with his followers through his 'Mo' letters. The roots of the sect were in Huntington, California, with Teens for Christ founded in 1968. It was later that they became known as the 'Children of God.' By 1972 this growing movement had about 300 communes in different parts of the world. One of their communes, populated by converted hippies, was in Bromley, South London.

This is where the group at Windsor Park had travelled from. This was the first time I had encountered the Children of God.

I learned later that, at first, the Christian community in Bromley had welcomed the Children of God because of their evangelistic work among the hippies. Local churches supported them and gave them premises in which to live and from which to work. Later, however, the Christian community denounced them after it became apparent that their syncretism with the prevalent permissive society had mortally corrupted the Christian values they claimed to live by.

To David Berg where the Bible says, "*To the pure, all things are pure*"[13] this meant everything including sex and nudity. Berg, the self-styled prophet, wrote over 3000 'Mo' letters and exerted a strong influence on his followers. By 1974 one method of evangelism he promoted was called "flirty fishing". He encouraged female members of the sect to offer themselves as bait for the men the sect were attempting to evangelize. This was obviously a corrupted reinterpretation of Jesus' words, "*I will make you fishers of men.*" Two guys from the Children of God had noticed me. Soon they would engage me in conversation.

A few years earlier when I was living in Rhyl, a friend introduced me to real Christians at a Saturday night youth event run by Sussex Street Baptist Church. By real Christians, I mean not just Christians in name only. They were distinct from some ritual churchgoers I had been familiar with as a child at church. These people followed a prayer book liturgy on Sunday, but their lives and conversation appeared to be indistinguishable to that of anyone else for the rest of the week. These Christians at Sussex Street had some life about them, and they really believed in what they were saying and doing.

It was the son of the chef at the YMCA holiday

centre, Roy, who invited me along. A short sermon took place at the end of the youth event - an epilogue of sorts. One evening Ray Hardway gave the epilogue. It was a preach from the Book of Revelation on the text, "*Behold I stand at the door and knock. If anyone opens the door, I will come in….*"[14]. Ray appealed to us to receive Jesus into our hearts as we were all invited to close our eyes for a prayer at the end. I received some kind of spiritual awakening that night but tried as best as I could to hide the fact from everyone around me, I was praying the prayer. It was real, but I was less than half-hearted about following this up. There was too much to give up if I were to be wholehearted about living the Christian life. All this came flooding back to me as two American guys from the Children of God began speaking to me. I didn't know it, but I was on the verge of the most extraordinary encounter. The single most life-changing event I have ever experienced was about to take me in an entirely different direction.

THE PARADIGM SHIFT

You see a maiden, I see a witch,
But just when you've seen it the image can switch.
You see a rabbit, I see a duck,
Your stairs go downwards, my stairs go up.

How do I know if I'm wrong and you're right?
When the truth you're describing is hidden from sight.
It's the same as your outlook surveying the land,
The picture you see will depend where you stand.
(Nigel E. Heath February 2019)

https://commons.wikimedia.org/wiki/File:My_Wife_and_My_Mother-in-Law.jpg (Public Domain)
https://archive.org/details/popularsciencemo54newy
Wikimedia Commons (Public Domain)

My first reaction to these two American "Jesus people" was to want to avoid them. There was a 'squeaky cleanness' about them that made me feel uncomfortable (this said more about me than it did about them). I had been busy collecting litter into large plastic bin bags. There were no bins, and people had scattered litter all over the place. I believed in our cause and followed my conviction. We should support our objectives for a better world and tidy up after ourselves rather than leave this to someone else. This was my way of promoting a good image and reputation for us hippies. It could increase the possibility that the authorities would permit free pop festivals at Windsor Park in the future.

I stopped to listen to these two guys as they engaged me in straightforward Christian evangelism. Jesus loved me, they told me, and I needed Jesus to go heaven. The Jesus people sang this cheesy song to acoustic guitar: "*Got to be baby... got to be a baby... got to be a baby to go to heaven*". I had heard them singing it earlier in the day. They were attempting to simplify the words of Jesus into language people could understand. The lyrics was based on the texts, "*unless you are born again, you cannot see the Kingdom of God*"[15] and "*unless you change and become like little children, you will never enter the kingdom of heaven*"[16].

Some conversation I remember vaguely, but other parts vividly. I recalled how, in the past, I nearly became a truly committed Christian when I heard the gospel at the youth event in Rhyl. My response to these two guys was to tell them my ambitions. Our hippie commune intended to save up and buy a place of our own, live off the land and drop out of society. But these guys countered with a compelling story of their own. They told me they had left farmlands in America to engage in what they were doing now. I replied that I reckoned within about four months' time we would have enough money to buy some kind of smallholding, with sufficient land to live our dream. One guy had a Bible with him and was very familiar with it. He told me he had a verse for me, and read from John's Gospel, "*Do you not say, 'There are yet four months, then comes the harvest'? Look, I tell you, lift up your eyes, and see that the fields are white for harvest.*"[17] Four months? The Bible said that instead of waiting four months, why don't you take this new opportunity now?

I tried to hide from them just how much all of this was getting through to me, and how my sincerely held position was being challenged. My worldview began to change. I was now seeing things differently and faced a choice. I knew that if I walked away, I would walk away a hypocrite. In having farmlands in America, they had enjoyed everything I was seeking, and they left it all behind to tell people like me about Jesus.

I stood there, deeply conflicted. I felt a strong pull to turn my back on them and walk away. But how could I live with myself? On the other hand, what was I letting myself in for if went along with what they were saying? I could not have explained it then. Only with the benefit of hindsight did I understand better. I had grown to believe so much in hippie ideals that I had become an evangelist for the cause. Now I was seeing things differently. I had got it wrong. Hippie ideology would not change the world. I still wanted to change the world for the better. Now I saw that the only true change-maker was Jesus. He alone had done something that worked. For me to be a real change-maker for good, I had to give my life to Jesus and allow him to do through me what no-one else could do. What was I going to do? Walk away a hypocrite, or give my life to Jesus?

Somehow, intuitively, I knew that if I gave my life to Jesus the way ahead would be very difficult, but I made my decision. "*What do I do? How do I do it?*" I asked. They suggested that I kneel there and then in the open air, and tell Jesus that I was a sinner, and ask Jesus into my life. In my head I was thinking, "*I'm not a sinner*". I hadn't a clue what it meant to be a sinner. But I went along with it anyway and said the words and asked Jesus into my life. Outwardly and inwardly it was publicly humiliating, but I had made the choice. This was one of the most difficult things I have ever done. I didn't realize how proud I was until that moment. It was the hardest thing to admit that I had been wrong. Tears were streaming down my face. Something irreversible took place in me. In Christian-speak, the language I would later learn, I had been "*filled with the Holy Spirit*". I knew already that something powerful had happened. Something had changed.

I didn't know what to do next. All I knew was that, having made this decision and prayed this prayer, I had discovered that Jesus was real. A rock band was in concert, so I went over to the cordon that separated the crowd from the performers. The guy next to me handed me a joint. I drew the smoke in deeply, but its effect was not what I expected. Instead of the buzz I would normally get, I experienced a kind of splitting of my mind, which is difficult to describe. Either way, I didn't like it and couldn't smoke it. So I gave him the joint back. I went back to the Jesus People and agreed to help distribute their leaflets. As I was handing these out, I came across the 'spooky' group. They were creepy people, standing and sitting around the grey ashes of a large campfire that had been burning in the night. Mixed in with the charcoal and ashes were the charred remains of a burnt animal. It looked as though they had offered ritual sacrifices during the previous evening. Together with this was a smell - no ordinary smell, but one resembling something like sulphur and death. I don't think it was a literal smell. It was more of a sense than a smell.

The leader of the group was the creepiest of all. He had a tattoo in the centre of his forehead, and he looked as though he embodied a personality that didn't fit. I imagined him having curled up toes. He had a dark, indistinguishable expression on his face. "*Stay away from him*", someone from the Children said; "*He carries a really evil vibe*". He came toward me. He had something in his hand - some kind of leaflet. I determined to give him my leaflet. As we exchanged leaflets, he opened his arms to me, inviting a hug. I complied, and it was then that something horribly sinister took place. It was as though, in the embrace, an exchange took place, with a transfer of the demons of hell finding a passage from him to me, taking up residence in my deepest spirit. I felt horribly contaminated. The experience traumatized me. No sooner had I chosen to join the Jesus people, and experienced God in the way I had, I was now experiencing something very different. I felt as though I had grown fangs like some kind of vampire and bore an evil grimace when I smiled.

The folks from the Children of God witnessed this. They saw that something had gone seriously wrong. I was in a mess. They let me into someone's van and gave me a set of headphones to listen to a Christian ministry tape. I found this soothing. I remember that it had become windy, and the van was rocking from side to side in the wind. One of them tried to help by reading to me a Bible verse: "*Whoever misleads the upright into an evil way will fall into his own pit*".[18] I kept repeating the text over and over in my mind. I hoped that by believing it strongly enough, I could reverse what the creepy guy had done to me. It would flip back onto him, and I would be free. However, the new unwelcome residents in my spirit made themselves at home. All of this is exactly as I recall it, with no exaggeration or embellishment.

From that time on, I was in a terrible state. I was already in poor health before my encounter with the man with the tattooed forehead. After this, my health deteriorated further. I was a cocktail of maladies. I had psychotic episodes, delusions of grandeur, and developed an obsessive-compulsive disorder. I became aware of gradually losing my ability to understand what people were saying. I was fast fading into a frightening world of further, disintegrating health and increasing isolation.

PSYCHOSIS

Whole, healthy and sound...
Distorted, bent and broken
Recovered, restored.

(Haiku - Nigel E. Heath February 2019)

T his will be the most difficult chapter to write. In total contrast to the dreadful events I must revisit, today I am on holiday. Just now, I am relaxing on a sunbed in Goa under the shade of a large poolside parasol. It is 31 degrees centigrade. It is February 2019, but in Goa there is bright sunshine and a cloudless sky. I am 67 years old, retired and content. I am married to a good woman. We have two very different sons, both of whom we are very proud. I have had a fruitful and fulfilling career, and when we return from holiday, I will not be idle. I will resume ministry with pre-scheduled preaching engagements and take up other invitations for Christian service.

Recalling memories of my traumatic experience at Windsor Park, it is difficult for me to work out what was happening. A medic might say I became mentally ill, and a Christian might say I became demonized. Perhaps both are true. You can come to your own conclusion as to what happened. It doesn't matter to me. This was without doubt the winter solstice of my life; the darkest of days.

At Windsor Park I had no money. I scrounged a few shillings from a nun - just enough to help me on my way back to Harold Road, Walthamstow where we were living. Harold Road was hardly a commune - just a group of us staying together: Frank and Dee, John and Jenny and another couple whose names I have forgotten. I was on my own. Life was not the same. I didn't know what to do.

To pass the time, I decided to make some cowslip wine. While I was separating the flowers from the stems, someone passed me a joint. Having had a bad experience the last time I took a smoke, I was wary of trying it again. I drew on it until the hit, but the same splitting of my mind occurred. My thoughts became distorted and delusional. As I processed the cowslip flowers, I began to think I was doing more than just separating petals from stems. I imagined I had developed the gift of sympathetic magic and was separating the wheat from the chaff. I was a powerful magician, a white warlock, with the capacity to make changes for good. As I pulled the blooms from the stalks, I was separating good from evil in a way that helped and healed the world. That's hard to understand if you haven't experienced it. It was confirmation that I could no longer smoke dope.

I will be forever indebted to a young guy from the Children of God in Bromley. He had my address, and he followed up my accepting of Christ into my life at Windsor Park with a letter. There is only one line in the letter I remember, *"Just tell Jesus that you love him"*. I wanted to, but it was very plain to me I couldn't say this and mean it without choosing to live in a way consistent with it. Something had happened to me the instant I knelt in the park and asked Jesus into my life. A powerful, irreversible transformation had begun. There was no going back. With very little money in my pocket and only the clothes I stood in, I said goodbye to my friends and left. I had chosen to follow Jesus, and the first step was to be on my way to Bromley, to join the Children of God.

The Children couldn't cope with me. I turned up and sensed that, having spoken with me and witnessed my condition, they had convened an impromptu prayer gathering in the room next door. As they prayed, it was as though they were attempting an exorcism. It felt like there was a kind speech bubble full of demons being squeezed from my inner spirit. I felt there was a point of attachment, but I refused to let go. What if the powers that had contaminated me harmed them instead?

There was no place for me with the Children

of God. That Sunday evening, a visitor to the Children took me to the local church. We walked into a church service part way through. After the service, a few people took me to someone's home. We stood at the doorstep, and when the door opened, I was introduced to them as "*a person who was very sick*". It is weird hearing yourself being described in this way. I felt detached, as though the person was someone else, whilst knowing it was me.

The kind, but firm gentleman gave me hospitality in his home. I was allowed to have a bath, with clear instructions on how to clean the bath afterwards. He offered me some food. "*I am a vegetarian,*" I said. I had been a vegetarian since the day some cattle approached us in a field near Hereford. We were high on acid, and it was a boiling summer's day. I was wearing leather sandals and a young bull approached me, lowering its head within inches of my sandals, sniffing with its steaming, flared and dripping nostrils. This was curiosity on the part of the young bull, but on an acid trip my perception was skewed. I interpreted the bull's behaviour to mean that the bullock was pointing out to me I was wearing animal skin belonging to its species. Terrified, I felt not only the threat of the surrounding herd of cattle, but a sense that the young bullock disapproved of my attire. I feared it would attack me, so I made a secret bargain there and then. If the cattle would leave us alone, I would no longer eat meat. My Christian host insisted that I ate some meat, and that it was okay to do so as a Christian. He quoted me chapter and verse about all foods being clean, and that I could eat with a free conscience. I remember him commenting that my diet was a probable contributory cause to my poor condition of health.

days later my hosts were to travel to Birmingham to an O.M. (Operation Mobilisation) conference. Did I want to come? Before arriving in Bromley, I had set off with the resolve to leave everything behind to follow Jesus, and this seemed to me to be the next step. So, I agreed and went with them. To my astonishment, at this well attended Christian conference in Birmingham, there was someone there who knew me - Roy from Rhyl - the same Roy who had invited me to the Christian youth event several years earlier when I lived in Rhyl. Roy had joined O.M. to serve as a radio officer on board their ship, the Logos. The Logos sailed to ports around the world with Christian books and the team shared the message of the gospel with indigenous people at pre-arranged events.

Roy spotted me and came over. I instantly recognized him. He knew of a couple, John and Pauline, who intended to travel to Rhyl that weekend. A senior Christian worker at the conference recommended that I go home to my parents and get a job. I considered this a challenge. Previously, I had left home with a stubborn determination never to return. I had committed myself to the ideal of opting out of society and achieve the goal of living off the land. But now things had changed. I was now a follower of Jesus. The only thing that really mattered to me was that I did what Jesus said. I accepted the offer and the challenge and went with them.

Reflecting on all of this, my conversion, a new direction and eventual recovery were all dependent on a succession of constructive interventions from others. A Jamaican preacher, evangelists at a pop festival, and someone who cared to write a letter were all instrumental. Others played their part, inviting me to church, inviting me into their home and taking me to a Christian youth meeting when I was a teenager. There was someone to challenge and advised me, and someone who offered me a lift home. What if one of them had chosen differently? What might have happened to me?

Only those who knew me or had encountered me during this period of my life can appreciate how dreadful my state of health had become. I am not sure what my parents thought when they first saw me after John and Pauline dropped me off at home. They could tell that something was seriously wrong. They appeared to confuse my poor condition of mental health with my newfound faith. I can understand them thinking I had developed some kind of religious mania.

I attended a local church and began reading the Bible from Genesis to Revelation. All I had was a small A.V. (Authorised Version). There was something not quite right with my vision. I recall seeing double for a while when I tried to read. Adjusting back to normality and recovering good health seemed unreachable, and although I hoped that I might one day get well again, I doubted this would ever happen. Had I caused irreversible brain damage through experimentation and excess? The thought crossed my mind.

You may sometimes see people walking the streets who have a mental illness. I was one of those people. I disliked Rhyl for years after, and I still do. People saw me in the streets manifesting obsessive-compulsive, bizarre behaviour. I still feel the stigma. I will mention a couple incidents that resulted from being driven by impulse and voices. These were not audible voices, but thoughts so strong that I felt an obligation to comply. I had read about fasting and prayer in the Old Testament. Old Testament characters, like Job's comforters, when they saw him,[19] heaped dust over their heads either in grief or in repentance. I had read of Moses going up the mountain to meet with God. I had learned about Jesus being led by the Spirit into the desert to be tempted. In my delusions of grandeur, I became convinced that if I went into the mountains to fast and pray for 40 days, I would trigger the second coming of Christ. This is what delusional psychosis is like. This is but one example of many I could recount. However, some memories are too painful to revisit and unnecessary to record.

On a late autumn evening in the dark, I set out for Mount Snowdon. My mission was to fulfil my duty to fast and pray in the mountains. My purpose was to bring about the second coming of Christ. I walked to Kinmel Bay, over the Foryd bridge and on for several miles. I then took a short-cut and cross the fields. It was dark by now and, unknown to me, the field I was crossing was full of cattle which became disturbed by my presence. There was a cow-shed in the middle of the field. I found my way into it. Walking to Snowdon was more difficult than I had thought, so I did what the old testament characters did, I would pray and repent in their style. There was no dust there, but there was plenty of cow dung. Yes, you guessed it; I heaped the cow dung over my head and body as I cried out to God. Nothing happened for the good. I had been making my way to Snowdon to fast and pray and change the world. Now I was stuck in a cowshed in a field full of mooing, snorting cattle in the cold and dark of night, and covered in cow dung. In a moment of lucidity, a shaft of light penetrated the darkness of my disturbed and deluded mind. I saw that God had not called me to pray and fast on Mount Snowdon at all.

I started back along the road I had taken. I cannot recall how far I had walked, but it was several miles. Fortunately for me, a car driver saw me, and must have recognized that I was in difficulty. The driver stopped and offered me a lift. What must the car must have been like after I left it? What a kind soul, whom I can never repay. I explained to him what had happened to me, and that I was thinking about going to the GP the following day. Somewhat understated, I recall him saying that he thought that would be a good idea.

The GP prescribed an antipsychotic drug named Largactil and advised me to remain at home. The GP wrote "nervous debility" on my record - probably to preserve my future prospects for employment. From what I have since learned I think "psychosis", or perhaps "psychotic episodes" may well have been nearer to the truth.

This was not the first psychotic episode I experienced. Neither would it be the last. I remember the first episode in detail. It was in Windsor Park at the pop festival not long after I had become contaminated through the demonic hug. Though onlookers may stare incredulously at those whose bizarre behaviour is without explanation, to the deluded mind everything makes sense. The Children of God owned a large coach. It was my intention to travel back with them to Bromley where they were staying. While in their company, and in the open park, a thought entered my mind. Could it be possible that there and then, by my example and brave intervention, I could trigger an event that would transform the festival into a Garden of Eden? Somehow, in my deranged thinking, I became convinced that singularly I had the power to do this. By taking a decisive step I could bring to fulfilment that illusory, better world us hippies longed for. But this would require faith and courage on my part. I sensed I could accomplish this if I were to strip naked there and then. Others would follow my example and do the same. We would feel no shame and would begin to transform the world.

This went strongly against my nature. I am no exhibitionist. But driven by the conviction and the enticement of the reward, I began to strip. The Children soon realized what was happening. I remember them desperately trying to persuade me to stop. *"You're listening to the devil"*, they said. They did everything in their power to dissuade me. But slowly, hesitantly yet resolutely, I just kept on stripping, right down to my underpants. It was then that I paused for a moment before finally taking them off and standing there in Windsor Park stark naked before the bewildered onlookers. And guess what - No one else stripped, and I did not restore Eden! Instead, the Children of God hurried unceremoniously onto their bus as fast as they could and made a swift getaway. They blocked my way onto the bus, making sure that I did not travel with them. In this most embarrassing of moments the only single comment I recall hearing from the otherwise silent, staring crowd was that of a young lady who exclaimed, *"Can't be bad!"*

Having experienced psychotic episodes, I appreciate how dangerous this can be. Months later, at my parent's home, I continued to have these episodes. I had been reading the Bible story of Gideon, who had first to prove himself by destroying his father's idol before he could become a person of influence with God. Gideon summoned up the courage and, in the night, he destroyed his father's altar to Baal and Asherah in the courtyard of their home.[20] I wondered what this might mean for me.

As I thought about this, obsessional compulsive thoughts gathered like storm clouds in my mind all over again. What was the equivalent of an altar to Baal in our household? What was my father's idol? What did Dad value more than God? What was it that God might have me destroy to prove my faith and worth? It was the dog. Chico was the tiny chihuahua Dad bought for Mum when we were in Nottingham. Dad doted on Chico. What might I have to do? You will be glad to know that no harm befell the wee creature.

I wondered if I would ever recover and doubted my prospects for there being any future for me. Would I ever find a Christian girlfriend? Would I ever be able to carry out practical tasks or finding gainful employment? Would there be anything worth living for? The worst symptom was my inability to make sense of what people were saying. Hearing the words was not the problem. Understanding what they meant was my difficulty. I created a kind of mental recording loop in my mind. Repeatedly going over the spoken words eventually enabled me to make sense of even the simple of statements. This meant there was often a long delay before I could reply. Imagine how difficult it was to book a train ticket over the phone or follow a simple conversation. People would repeat themselves and ending up shouting as though I was deaf. After my recovery, I developed great sympathy for people with illnesses of the mind.

I remained convinced that in Windsor Park

I had been demonised through contact with the spectre who had the tattooed forehead. No-one appeared to have either the skill or courage to carry out an exorcism on me. This led me to commit to a full seven-day fast, taking no water for the first three days. This was my sincere appeal to God in faith, for deliverance. It proved to be a turning point. I experienced a critical measure of deliverance. Others commented on it. A full recovery of my mind, however, would be a gradual process. It took years and much hard work. Dad didn't take it too well when I told him I intended to stop my medication and trust the Lord for healing. His response was that if I did, he would have me forcibly committed to a mental hospital. Though I would not recommend others to stop their medication in circumstances like mine, it was right for me. Even my G.P. agreed that my faith was helping me. My presence in the home must have been a nightmare for my parents. I had little interaction with them. Dad was distant as usual. He found no way to connect with me, nor I with him. I struggled to forgive him for hurting me so deeply. It became a choice. Choosing to forgive is one thing, but sometimes the wounds from hurts run so deep that warmth and affection become cauterized beyond recovery. I wished it were otherwise.

Mum went about things the way Mum did. She left a book on the table in the lounge on the subject of obsessive-compulsive behaviour, with the title facing upwards to catch my eye. Both my parents are now gone, having lived into their late 80s. Mum faded away with dementia, and Dad withered away with heart failure. I would love to have them back for a day to talk with them. I could speak to them as an experienced adult of pensionable age. Oh, to have those conversations with them I wish had taken place when they were still alive and with me, but never did! I could boast of the achievements of our now grown-up sons. I could tell them of the joy the grandchildren have brought into our lives.

Obsessive behaviour had its advantages. I determined to right as many wrongs as I could think of; paying back people from whom I had taken things and apologising to others I had hurt. I determined to work the six days the Commandments required for us to labour. I became self-employed, working as a window cleaner, having made an improvised cart out of an old pram, this time to transport ladders. The physical exercise helped towards my recovery. Later I began an apprenticeship in Radio, TV and Electronics. The mental agility required to think logically, and to use reason was a challenge but one which further helped my recovery. Faith, prayer and long, long hours of study into the late evening every night were essential for me to succeed. Dedicated, focussed and determined, with God's kind intervention and healing, I was now on the mend.

It was soon possible for me to take a few driving lessons and pass my driving test first time. I also started work as a TV engineer. However, I developed a nagging, growing sense of call to some form of overseas Christian missionary work. My pastor advised me that Bible college training was an essential first step. I had no money, there were no student loans, and government grants were discretionary. Although there was no guarantee of a grant, I applied in faith and I handed in my notice to the boss at work. Three days before the course at Lebanon Missionary Bible College in Berwick-upon-Tweed began, I received a letter stating that my application for college fees and accommodation costs had been successful. I leapt in the air for joy. Someone somewhere had used their discretion in my favour. A new butterfly effect intervention opened the way for me. A new chapter was about to begin.

A NEW SEASON

THE HERALD OF NEW HOPE
The sweet song of a blackbird in the early morning,
Beckons through the gap in my open window,
Calling me from slumber to witness a new dawning,
I listen to its song of hope with my head upon my pillow.

Summoned by the Herald of New Hope
I dress quietly in the dark
To witness for myself the emergence of a new beginning.
And stepping into nature's dawn I sense and see that
brighter, warmer, lengthening days have made their
mark,
As other birds join with the blackbird's singing.

The sun has yet to rise at this last hour of the night,
But soon it will appear on the horizon.
Within the orange, red and azure pastel shades its light
and rays will pierce the darkness like a diamond.

Winter now belongs to yesterday.
A new season has begun.
Buds are poised to open, and bees awaken.

And I have found new hope
in the promise of the blackbird's song.

(Nigel E. Heath February 2019)

A t the time of writing, the early spring of 2019 is approaching. The clocks go forward this weekend and the evenings will be longer. I have yet to hear the blackbird's song this season, but I have been keeping my window open at night in anticipation of hearing it before dawn. Poets and writers sometimes allegorize the seasons of the year to represent the seasons of life: birth, budding youth, blossoming and fruitfulness, fading, ageing and death. It is the season of spring that I like the most. Winter is behind us and warmer, brighter, longer days that I associate with hope, lie ahead.

1976-1979 marked the start of a new spring season of life and hope for me. These were three years spent studying at Lebanon Missionary Bible College. Berwick itself is a town with an interesting history. Its origin was as an Anglo-Saxon settlement. Later it became a border town between England and Scotland that changed hands frequently depending on which of the kingdoms, north or south was in the ascendency. D.W. Lambert founded the college and 1946, and the Lamberts named in it to match their vision for its future. The college had no link with Lebanon the country. Its name came from the Bible text, "*From the wilderness and this Lebanon even unto the great river, the river Euphrates, all the land of the Hittites, and unto the great sea toward the going down of the sun, shall be your coast.*"[21] The landscape of the area fits well with the text. In faith, they expected the college to prosper, and in the years that followed, it did.

It was on a foul, wet September day that I set off from Rhyl to travel to Berwick-upon-Tweed for the first day of term at Lebanon Missionary Bible College. I was travelling north on the M6 riding a twin-cylinder Yamaha 250cc two-stroke motorcycle. My comparatively small, but faithful bike was loaded heavily with everything I needed, firmly strapped to the back, and I was pushing it a bit. Suddenly, near to Keswick, the bike lost power and clouds of black smoke poured out from the exhaust pipe. I limped into Keswick and parked up outside a motorcycle spares shop and prayed.

Fortunately, I had a tool kit with me. On stripping down the top end of the engine I discovered a molten hole burnt right through the centre of an alloy piston. The engine had reached such a high temperature that the alloy had melted. The shop didn't have the part, but next door to the spares shop there was a welder who agreed to repair the piston with an alloy plug. By this time the rain clouds I had passed through on my journey north had caught up with me. I put the bike back together in the pouring rain and tried to kick-start it. The bike roared into life, and I was on my way.

This set me back a good number of hours. By the time I arrived in Berwick, it was late at night. The Student Chairman greeted me as I arrived soaking wet, weary and with my hands covered in black grease. He told me to tread quietly along the edge of the corridor so as not to waken the students. The dormitory corridor floorboards were very creaky.

A regimented, almost Victorian culture characterised the day to day running of the College. I shared a twin room with one other student. Lectures took place in the morning. There were strict daily study times in the afternoon and also in the evening from 6 p.m. to 9 p.m. Students laid the table for breakfast, supervised by Miss Bonner. She was a former housekeeper from the Scottish Highlands - always prim and proper with her hair tied in a bun. Everyone turned up on time. Someone said grace, and the students and staff together devoured the freshly made oatmeal porridge, soaked overnight, and prepared that morning in the kitchen under the supervision of Miss Bonner. Mandatory at breakfast, we listened each morning to the BBC world news. The college had no television.

There were duty rotas for everything - dishes, setting tables, cleaning public bathrooms and toilets, dusting and vacuuming. In addition, students took part in colportage, door-to-door witness, and church services on Sundays, mostly in local Methodist churches. Dress was formal - collar, tie and jacket for the guys and skirts for the ladies.

No-one went to the pub. One wag had famously re-named L.M.B.C. as the *"Lonely Maids and Bachelor's Club"*. This was not without good reason. Many a romance started there. Whilst it was a good place to meet and get to know people, it was difficult for couples to risk starting a relationship in the open forum of student life. Gossip was rife, and if relationships went pear-shaped, there was nowhere to hide.

My original intention in going to Bible College was to join the W.E.C.[22] Inspiration for this came from my first church pastor and his wife, Charlie and Lily Searle in Kinmel Bay near Rhyl. They were a remarkable former missionary couple who had worked in the then Belgium Congo (now Zaire), having gone out there in 1928. Charlie told many a story of times on the "mission field". He recalled early memories of meeting the founder of the W.E.C., C. T. Studd in the Congo. This meeting must have taken place within the first three years of Charlie's first tour of service because C.T. Studd died of untreated gall stones in 1931 when in Ibambi.

Charlie was a diminutive man with a neat moustache - a regular 'pocket battleship' with a perhaps more than slightly choleric temperament and prone to thumping the pulpit when he preached. Lily was a kind, gentle, hospitable lady who often invited me over to enjoy some of her home-made broth for lunch. I can still hear her welcoming voice, *"Come away in"*. Charlie and Lily were both highly committed Christians with broad experience and a shared zeal for overseas mission.

Before entering college, I had settled into work in the television trade as a bench technician in Colwyn Bay. Dad was about to take another YMCA job and move to Caerphilly in South Wales. When they broke the news to me, I realized that my going with them was not part of the plan. Dad did what he could to arrange for me to move into a bedsit before they left. The place was foul - a single room with a single bed and a Baby Belling electric ring to cook on. There were stains on the blankets. The room had no extractor fan, and the odour of stale cabbage from years of unvented cooking fumes permeated the dated wallpaper and fabric of the room. There was a single shared bathroom and toilet on the landing that some other lodgers often left in a disgusting state.

I travelled into work each day on a Honda 50 motorcycle. Being poorly paid, I had very little money left at the end of each month. Rent, basic food, fuel for the bike and a tithe left me with no ability to save. I moved from the bedsit to take up kind offers of hospitality in the homes of older church members. This never worked out. It was good of them to host me, but I cannot imagine I was an easy lodger. I would have preferred to live independently. Better still, married.

From the moment of my conversion, I was keen to tell others about Jesus. Their lives could be so much better if they put their trust in Christ. Christ had made such a difference for me. Jesus powerfully transformed my life from within. Having discovered this, I wanted others to experience God's power through the gospel to transform their lives, circumstances, and relationships. They too could enjoy freedom from guilt and the hope of heaven. What was mine could be theirs. This has always held far greater appeal to me than attempts to improve the circumstances of others at a mere surface, superficial level. A shallow approach compares to using sticking plasters to cover over the symptoms of a disease that requires deep, radical surgery to effect a cure.

It is easy to understand from these insights and disclosures that one day I dared to dream that I could serve as a missionary; possibly in Africa. Others had encouraged me to think about this - not least the people I worked with. They could see what I had set my heart on. Africa had always attracted me. It still does. I love African people and gravitate towards them wherever and whenever I see them. I sometimes joke with them and tell them I am an African in disguise. It could be because I spent my early childhood in Cameroon.

I have a few childhood memories of Africa and those I have are mostly good. As children, we had two donkeys named Jerusalem and Bethlehem. Sometimes we rode them. It must have been in Africa that I developed a fascination for insects and wildlife. There was a great variety, including a civet cat that would prowl on the roof at night, and bats that soon appeared after sunset.

These memories have caused me at times to question my motives for going to Africa. Did I really have a "call" to serve God in Africa? Or did I just like the thought of returning there?

Christians talk about the "call of God" to Christian service, but how well do Christians understand what this is? In my opinion, it can be over-spiritualized. Do we not experience the call of God to non-sacred vocations? Olympic champion Eric Liddell made more famous through the 1981 film "Chariots of Fire" said, "God made me fast. ... And when I run, I feel his pleasure." This sounds to me like a calling.

Eric Liddell was born in China to missionary parents who had responded to a different sense of call. But both Eric Liddell and his parents lived as committed Christians in their own way. My understanding of a sense of call to full-time, paid or supported Christian work is that it is often more of a developing conviction than a blinding light. I believe that God expects us to be more active than passive, and to try a succession of doors one by one to see if they open. Should one door open then we can choose to go further and try the next door until the final door yields and circumstances confirm the direction we have taken.

Life for me continued to improve. By the time I started Bible college I had made a significant but not a full recovery from my illness. Reading and study at college remained intensely difficult. The theological content of the Cambridge Certificate/Diploma course was liberal and academic. This did not help, as I was not unaccustomed to my evangelical beliefs being challenged. Well defended, I had an aversion to reading and absorbing anything that threatened to erode the strong faith fortifications I had assembled. At the time, I lacked the capacity to process critical studies in a way that strengthened my faith rather than threatened it. However, I made it through and gained a pass at Certificate level as well as gaining the college diploma.

Reflecting again on the butterfly effect, without a doubt the most pivotal moment of my life was when I stood in the open in Windsor Park and considered the choice. Would I follow Christ or go my own way? As I weighed the options, I was unaware that my whole future hung in the balance. From that point on, everything that followed would depend on my decision. Had I walked away, what might my life have become? Perhaps a short-lived ruin; I will never know. The paradox is that I thought by following Christ I was giving away everything. In a sense, I did. However, in the long-term I gained so much more. I never intended this, and it is only in retrospect that I now see how my exchange was one of rags for riches.

Right from the moment of my conversion I gained a sense of purpose for living that, prior to this, I had always lacked. The early years of my Christian faith were the most difficult. These years were the most intensive period of my recovery. I don't think many people realize just how traumatic conversion to Christianity can be. It was for me. I left my friends and the world I knew behind me and navigated a strange culture with an unfamiliar language. Christian vocabulary, sometimes described as "Christianese", was part of this strange new world. However, I found acceptance and a sense of belonging within the Christian community. But I soon discovered that not all Christians are the same. Churches were different too, and Christians didn't all believe the same things.

Initially, I sensed that to have people accept me fully into this new faith community, in addition to accepting Christ, I would have to agree with all their beliefs. The professed beliefs of some of them appeared to be fundamentalist and even obscurantist. How was I going to square their very literal interpretation of the early chapters of Genesis, with the theory of Evolution I had been brought up to believe to be the truth? I lacked confidence and was afraid of getting things wrong. So, at first, I ignored my intuitive quest for the whole truth. Instead of questioning what I was being taught, I accepted all of it. Later in life, and with the benefit of study and deeper insight, I discovered that credible truth and the Bible rightly interpreted do not contradict scientific fact at all. I learned to interpret the truth of the Bible correctly. Correct interpretation involved taking into consideration the genre of the different books of the Bible. In the Bible there are books of poetry as well as prose. There is a myth genre as well as factual historical record. I still rarely use the word "myth" among Christian friends to describe a

Bible genre. I fear that some Christians may either misunderstand or even rejected me for my use of the word myth. By myth, I do not mean fiction or fables or the equivalent of fairy stories with no divine inspiration. Myth in the Bible is truth stated in a particular writing style - a genre.

It saddens me that some Christians, out of misguided loyalty, feel pressured to promote as truth something that is at least unlikely to be true. A typical example is young earth theory. Some Christians insist that the Bible teaches the world was created literally in six 24-hour day periods of time and is only 6000 years old. Given the myth genre of these chapters in Genesis, an over-literal interpretation is unnecessary.

Don't get me wrong, I believe that Jesus Christ is the Son of God, born of the Virgin Mary, performed miracles and literally rose again after his death by crucifixion. The Gospels and the Book of Acts are of a different genre. They include historical records of events that took place at the time that are rightly understood as literal, factual and true according to their genre. My faith remains firmly in Christ as the one who took the judgement for all that my sin deserved. And for me, the only credible explanation for the powerful, spiritual experience of conversion that I had at Windsor Park is that this encounter was with Christ who lives - the Christ I have known, loved and been loved by from that time until now.

Life at L.M.B.C., though a dream come true, was a steep learning curve. I had originally been interested in working with W.E.C. International but noticed another opportunity to serve in Nigeria at a mission hospital with Qua Iboe Mission (now Mission Africa). The hospital needed someone with practical skills who would be capable of carrying out maintenance and development work. This was very appealing to me. I was in my final year at college and another development was taking place. I spied a certain lady - Elizabeth (Liz, as she preferred to be known) and I dared to ask her out to dinner. She accepted.

Living in the college fishbowl, observed by all the students, turned out to be not as bad as I imagined. We expected our two paths to merge and form a single path towards a common goal and future. Liz too, as a State Certified Midwife, could see herself serving at a mission hospital abroad. On 23rd June 1979 we married in Larbert and our adventure together began.

> *"Green Pastures are before me*
> *Which yet I have not seen.*
> *Bright skies will soon be o'er me,*
> *Where the dark clouds have been.*
> *My hope I cannot measure,*
> *My path to life is free.*
> *My Saviour has my treasure,*
> *And he will walk with me."*

(Verse from "In Heavenly Love Abiding" by Anna Laetitia Waring 1850, and chosen as one of our wedding hymns)

PATHS MERGE

AFFECTION REFLECTION

My love for you is a mystery, a longing, a passion,
Stronger, greater, warmer than all loves that I have ever known,
Whether of cute puppy dogs, or the best of friends.
This love draws me to you. It never ends.

And can it be that the impossible is true?
That your love for me is as is mine for you?
A gift – affection shared together.
A dream come true, a passion shared forever.

I'm drawn to you. We share a smile, a kiss,
And time stands still, I want to linger here awhile.
For leaving your embrace too soon I'll miss.
You love me too. I see it in your smile.

Walk with me. I do not want to go alone.
You're by my side. I'm glad you're here.
Together for a lifetime, two as one,
I cannot say how wonderful it is to have you near.
(Nigel E. Heath May 2012)

L oneliness, as the lonely know, is living in the absence of longed-for, compassionate companionship. It is a void consistent with brooding, aching melancholy. I had often dwelt there, but my days of loneliness were ending. Liz and I got engaged, and we were married. I wore my wedding ring proudly, routinely putting it on each morning. I had completed college, but Liz still had one year to go.

We moved into a tiny Georgian flat in Berwick with sloping floors and low doorways. I took employment driving a large van delivering bread from Bryson's bakery to supermarkets in the surrounding Borders towns of Greenlaw, Kelso and other places on route. This meant rising at 3 A.M. or 4 A.M. It was an early start, but it paid a wage. Liz continued with her studies and took part-time work as a midwife in the local Castle Hills maternity hospital where every Berwick child was born. Sometimes our paths crossed in the early hours of the morning as Liz came home from a shift at work just as I was leaving.

I am not sure what Liz's family made of me to start with. News reached them that Liz was going out with an Englishman. He had a polite accent. This must have aroused curiosity. Finally, they met me and gradually got to know me. We invited Liz's brother Tom and his wife down to Berwick to have a meal with us. I enjoy a bit of cooking and I was the chef for the day. Jugged hare was on the menu. To Tom it probably sounded very posh, and the meal turned out to be not too bad.

After the meal Tom asked, "*Where did you get the hare from?*" I had thought nothing of it. I was driving Liz's pale blue VW Beetle (Herbie by name) down a narrow Berwickshire country road when a hare darted out from the hedgerow and glanced the front bumper. In my wing mirror I could see the blow had been fatal and that the hare was lying in the road, motionless. Mazal tov, as the Jews say. I had never tasted hare, so now was my chance.

This is the true nature of this "Englishman"; unashamed to take advantage of an opportunity. Whatever illusions Tom had about me, these were about to be quickly dispelled. Without a thought, I told Tom where it came from. I had served them roadkill without telling them and without think- ing it might be an issue for them. He never let me forget it. And I don't necessarily see myself as an "Englishman". I have little sense of national iden- tity and am happy to identify as an adopted Scot "gone native" having married a Scot and moved north of the border.

Considerable developments took place dur- ing the first eighteen months of our married life. Liz graduated with her Cambridge Certificate and Col- lege Diploma. We then moved to Falkirk, where I assisted Rev. Guy Finnie at Larbert Baptist Church. I earned extra money, again as a self-employed window cleaner. Part-time temporary employment was unavailable. All I needed was a temporary job to tide me over before we travelled to Nigeria with the Qua Iboe Mission to work at Ochadamu Medical Centre.

By now we were also expecting our first child, David.

David was born at Falkirk Royal Infirmary on 3rd October 1980. I was present at the birth. David was delivered using Kielland's forceps. He was a long, limp baby when he was born, probably because of the large quantities of Entonox Liz had been inhaling to help with the pains of childbirth. David soon roused, and it amazed me to watch this untaught little boy sneeze and yawn for the first time. It was like watching a miracle.

We soon discovered that David could have issues with his eyesight. At first, we noticed a slow, course, rolling nystagmus and brought this to the attention of the G.P. Later, medical staff confirmed that David had been born with ocular albinism. This would mean that, since there was a lack of pigment in his eyes, his sight would not develop fully. It came to us as a shock. His condition was both congenital and familial.

As parents of a newborn with a visual impairment, we didn't know what to do. Medics can be skilled at explaining a medical condition. They are not always as competent explaining the meaning of such a condition or advising what steps to take next. We received little guidance and had to take initiative ourselves. We learned that little that could be done, and no treatments were available. Undeterred, within three months of David's birth we had packed our belongings and were ready to leave for Nigeria.

Looking back on it now, in taking a step like this, we walked towards danger. But faith seems so much more straightforward when we are young. What could be safer than being in the centre of God's will? After a tearful farewell we set off on a flight to Lagos, Nigeria. It was difficult for Liz and her family to say goodbye to each other. Unlike me, with my family scattered and with no close ties to any group of friends, Liz's family had firm bonds. Born in Cowie and brought up in Bannockburn, family ties were close. We are grandparents now and can better appreciate how difficult it must have been for Liz's parents to watch their newborn grandchild carried away to a foreign land.

It was Sunday 18th January 1981 and a blanket of deep snow lay on the ground. I was excited. Liz was apprehensive. We travelled to the airport and took the flight. After long hours we finally stepped out into the overwhelming heat and humidity of the tropical air. I noticed what I thought to be the scent of the mangrove swamps seeping into the aircraft as we neared our destination. In some ways it felt to me like coming home. We made our way through customs with comparative ease. Then it was on by car, through the colour, noise, dust, smells and chaos of the Nigerian roads. We stayed locally overnight. The following day we took a ten-hour journey and arrived at Ochadamu. At Ochadamu was the medical centre compound where we would live and work for the next few years.

This was a new world for both of us. It was difficult to adjust at first. We hit the ground running. In a few days, I was off on a trip to Makurdi with the hospital chemist, and days later to Kano to collect medical supplies for the hospital. The reality for Liz of what it meant to be a "missionary" struck home early. Particularly in those first few weeks, the loneliness that I had once suffered became hers. Both David and Liz reacted badly to the new diet and climate, both succumbing to diarrhoea and vomiting, which lasted for a while until they adjusted to the conditions. Liz wrote in her diary, "*I really feel very, very low and upset and I can't lift myself out of it*". She so badly missed her family and friends and the familiarity of home. There is a 1970s worship song written by the Continentals with the line in it that goes, "*I want to be in service for Jesus; to win the lost, whatever may be the cost, I want to be in service for him*". We felt so spiritual, sincere and committed to the ideal of sacrificial service for God when we played the song before we left. It felt good. However, the painful reality of sacrificial living felt different. Christian service meant isolation, illness and homesickness. Together with tropical heat, humidity and with no air conditioning and a sick child, we no longer felt warm and fuzzy listening to the words of the song.

Although we took our prophylactics, we still got malaria. It's an unpleasant disease. I got to know the onset. As soon as the fever started, I took tablets to cure it because I knew that within an hour the vomiting would start. It left us incapacitated for days.

By far, our worst day out there was 17th July 1983. It's easy to remember because it was Liz's 34th birthday. David was not yet three years old. That morning, David took his tricycle outside and started riding around the house on the high veranda. He'd done it before, but this time we went too near to the edge and toppled over. We rushed out to see what had happened. David was crying and holding his arm. He couldn't bend it properly, so we went over to see Janet, the expatriate doctor to get his arm examined. Janet thought he may have dislocated his elbow. We had no X-ray equipment at the hospital. For that, we had to travel to Idah, 50km away. We took the journey and had David checked out. He needed no further treatment; just his arm in a sling and some rest.

We arrived back home two hours before sunset. Liz went into our tiny kitchen and started cooking. She poured some raw palm oil into a pan and placed the pan on the Calor Gas flame, covering it with the lid. Just then, a missionary colleague arrived at the open door to ask how David was. Distracted for a moment, Liz told her the story and then remembered the pan. She went quickly back into the kitchen and lifted the pan lid. By this time, it was smoking hot. It exploded into a fireball. Burning oil landed on the back of her hands and on her leg. She pivoted to rush to the outside standpipe and dowse it under running water. But as she turned, she slipped and fell on the burning oil which, by now, was all over the concrete floor. The burns were serious, and she needed a skin graft. The medical team got together and anaesthetized her with Ketamine before surgery. It took weeks to heal. Hardly a happy birthday. I couldn't believe how so much could go so wrong in just one day.

The group Casting Crowns have a song called "Heroes" which is about ordinary people who few people notice but are the true heroes. The chorus goes, "*These are the heroes, just ordinary people, laying down their lives like angels in disguise. They're weak, but always willing. They dare to do the hard things. And in the dark and desperate places no one else goes, You'll find the heroes*." Liz was the hero in Nigeria. Forget William Carey, the "*founder of modern missions*". Spare a thought for his dear wife Dorothy who, because of the rigours of living amidst the disease and isolation of life in India in the late 18th century, lost her mind and eventually her life. I'll leave you to judge who the true hero was.

Things gradually got better for us. It was easier when David became a toddler. David often accompanied me at work, riding with me on the saddle of my blue off-road sand motorcycle with its

squat tyres. Liz and I enjoyed quiet evenings together, playing scrabble. We listened to the same,
well-worn cassette tapes we had brought out with
us, against the background rumble of the diesel generator in the distance and the loud whistling of
crickets.

Reflecting on our experience of following the
call to mission, Liz undoubtedly made the greater
sacrifice. She bore the greater cost, even in her
willingness to return with me to Nigeria for a second tour after our first two-year assignment at
Ochadamu was completed. I was busy and out and
about each day enjoying the fulfilment of keeping
the medical centre functioning. Liz contributed in
other ways, taking care of the children for most of
the time. It was together as a couple that we had the
privilege of serving with the team out there, saving
lives, sometimes in the most extraordinary of circumstances.

Taken during our first tour in Nigeria at Ochadamu Medical
Centre 1981

WILD DANGER

L iving in Africa was an enriching experience that expanded my horizons. It was like seeing things in 3D after one-dimensional living in the U.K. There was both beauty and danger everywhere. Scented frangipani and magnificent Flame trees decked the compound. But concealed beneath were dangers from snakes, scorpions, centipedes and soldier ants. Statistically, we were in much greater danger of being killed on the roads than by some venomous creature. Wherever we travelled there were wrecks of vehicles and shrines at the roadside commemorating, the untimely end of some poor unfortunate. These served as a reminder to proceed with caution.

We were constantly on duty. I was often called upon to deal with a rat or a spitting cobra that had ventured into the home of a colleague. These creatures were easily dispatched with a long club, but not without taking necessary precautions to avoid getting venom in my eyes. Little brown scorpions were the sneaky ones. They would hide in crevices and unexpected places. In the morning, it was wise to knock out a pair of shoes before putting them on, just in case some insect was lurking there. A small, brown scorpion stung me when lifting a wet tarpaulin off some bricks during the rainy season. The pain was instant, travelling the full length of my arm from fingertip to shoulder. A medical colleague filled my finger with local anaesthetic to numb the pain, and this helped.

Snakes were a greater danger. Carpet vipers were particularly nasty. These are small, brown and beige patterned vertebrates difficult to see. They are well camouflaged against the undergrowth; hence the name. In the bush I wore ankle boots, but Africans went around mostly barefoot or wore only flat foam sandals and were much more vulnerable to being bitten.

People turned up at the dispensary at all times of day and night. We were the only local Accident and Emergency service for miles around. Patients turn up with all kinds of ailments, including snakebite. One day, a noisy group of people hurriedly carried a young man into the dispensary. Red, weeping burns covered his body from head to toe. He had been filling a petrol tank too near to a fire when it exploded, causing his injuries. On another occasion, a young man was carried in after being knocked down by a car. He had a broken femur. The admissions doctor asked if I could make an improvised Braun's splint for him with a sandbag weight to provide sufficient traction for the bone to realign and heal. I succeeded, following instructions from an old book. Sadly, days later he discharged himself, preferring to use the services of a tribal bone setter. His family took him away, and that was the last we saw of him.

Another time a dangerously ill young woman arrived at the hospital having suffered obstructed labour and who now had a ruptured uterus. The expatriate surgeon asked if I would take some discrete photographs of the surgery, and I obliged. Now, we didn't have a blood bank. No such thing in the Nigerian bush, and during the surgery the lady showed signs of having lost too much blood. My blood type is O rhesus positive, which is a very common blood group amongst Africans. A quick cross match showed that so was she. The next minute I was the blood donor providing a unit of blood for transfusion. Then I was up on my feet again, taking photos... I have a photo of the surgery which includes an IV bag on a drip stand with my blood in it. The lady survived. I saw her a few days later having recovered, and she looked remarkably well. Blood donors save lives every day. They just don't happen to be present at the point of delivery. For me, it was a privilege to see its value directly for myself.

Ochadamu Medical Centres was one of very few remote hospitals in the area. It served such a wide, scattered population that people arrived at the dispensary, sometimes before dawn, in large numbers. People came with malaria or other fevers.

Measles was a killer disease. Sometimes it developed into meningitis, particularly in malnourished children. People presented with strangulated hernias, filariasis, tuberculosis and leprosy (these were the years before the AIDS epidemic).

One day a Ghanaian teacher from the local school became worryingly ill. Remembering my experience, I saw in him the symptoms of psychosis. His behaviour became so bizarre that he was fast becoming a danger to himself. We knew local people might kill him if he continued to threaten the safety of the villagers.

The crisis came to a head when he became so disruptive that a group of us felt it necessary to overpower him - and he was strong. We bound his hands and feet with bandages to restrain him and carried him to a hospital bed. We did not have the luxury of specialist psychiatric units or places to which we could refer him. He complained that the bandages were too tight. We told him we would untie him on the condition that he allowed us first to give him an injection. Without questioning, he agreed. The doctor administered paraldehyde (which renders the patient unable to move) and we took the bandages off. But how would we deal with him?

We decided the best thing to do would be to take him to the central police station in Idah and explain the situation to them. They were very sympathetic and charged him with disturbance of the peace, having locked him in a holding cell for his own safety before his strength returned. We visited him regularly for the next couple of weeks to see if his condition would improve, but it didn't. The police could not keep him in a holding cell forever. They advised a course of action. It would be better for him to be found guilty in a court of law. Then they could send him to the local prison, where conditions were much better. I felt dreadful. I was the court witness, there to give evidence against this poor young man. My account of his behaviour would ensure that he was found guilty and imprisoned, but for his own good. I sensed he might not see it this way.

A surprising thing happened on the day I visited him at Idah prison. I met the prison governor there and mentioned that my father had been the prison advisor in Nigeria in the 1950s. The governor's stern appearance suddenly crumbled. Much to the surprise of his colleagues, how frowns gave way to smiles, excitement and delight. He hugged me and told me that my father had been his instructor when he was in training. "*He always dressed in immaculate white*", he said. It will please you to know that our young Ghanaian friend recovered not long after and was released from prison as soon as he did. He returned to Ochadamu, but then left for Ghana almost immediately.

Rarely a day went by without there being some unexpected event. During a storm one night, with a simultaneous flash and bang, lightning struck a tree next to the house, splitting the trunk.

Walking through the bush one afternoon, I found a chameleon. Superstition got the better of local Africans who ran in every direction when they saw me carrying it home. One night I got out of bed and ended up screaming like a little girl. I had to make an early start that day and rose well before dawn, putting on my dressing gown in the dark. As I did, I felt the presence of a large creature, hidden inside, scurrying up my back (it was only a gecko, but I imagined worse).

There was the occasional true emergency at the hospital. I was called in to assist now and again. A snake had bitten one of the leprosy patients and his gums had started bleeding. This confirmed he had been poisoned. We tried to find out what kind of snake had bitten him. He told us he'd been bitten while cutting cassava at his farm allotment. He had then killed the snake and thrown it into the bush. I searched the area to see if I could find it and identify it. Eventually I found it hanging on a low branch. It was a carpet viper.

The venom of a carpet viper causes the blood to lose its coagulant ability. Left untreated, sufficient venom causes the victim to die of internal bleeding. Our friend was losing blood and dying. We held no stocks of anti-venom. These were available only at the Idah hospital over an hour's drive away. But would there be any stock? We had no phones then to ring up and find out. Before I left for Idah, Charlie, the expatriate doctor and I, both O rhesus positive, agreed to give him blood. We didn't use an IV blood bag with anticoagulants in it. Instead, blood was drawn directly from our veins with a large syringe through a cannula. The assistant then injected the blood into the patient, with the needle being changed after each transfer. After donating blood, I set off in a hurry.

When I arrived at the hospital, I explained the urgency of the situation to a member of staff. In Nigeria, nothing happens in a hurry. I don't think they quite understood how critical the situation was. The staff member sent me down a corridor to where the stocks of snake antivenom were stored in a fridge inside a room. The door was locked, and the keyholder was absent. I thought to myself: there is a man dying at Ochadamu; there may be some snake anti-venom in the fridge in the room; this could save his life; the person with the key isn't here; the door looks flimsy. What do I do? Do I go back empty-handed? I am not authorized to break down the door. Should I do it anyway to save a life? Fortunately, I didn't have to make the choice. The person with the key arrived. He opened the door and looked inside the fridge. And yes, they had some anti-venom for a carpet viper bite, but there was insufficient for a full dose, and it was out of date. They gave me what they had, and I set off for Ochadamu in the pickup truck. I hurried along the dusty, bumpy roads in the night hoping to get back in time to save a life. I didn't know if was still living or had died. It may be hard to imagine a world without mobile phones, but we lived in one. There wasn't even a landline to connect Ochadamu Medical Centre to the outside world.

I arrived at the compound and parked up near to the ward. Entering the ward, I could see that he was still alive, but weak. Charlie administered the anti-venom, and we waited. I could see the fear in the man's eyes as he lay there facing the possibility of death. Gradually his condition stabilised, and the bleeding finally stopped. He had had a very close call, but over the next few days he gradually gained strength and finally made a full recovery. I met him years later when I returned to Nigeria in 2001 to take a STEP (Short Term Partnership) team on a visit. It was rewarding to hear him say in pidgin English, "If not for you and doctor I for die".

One afternoon, not long after his recovery, I met him down at the leprosy colony where he lived. He had been a resident there from early manhood after being excluded from his community when his family and other villagers learned of his condition. Nerve and muscle damage had disfigured his feet, hands and facial features ravaged by the disease before treatment had effected a cure. He asked me to follow him, and he took me to a damaged, discarded bedside locker on a rubbish heap nearby where wild bees had made a hive. I could hear the quiet hum of lines of bees entering and leaving through the crack in the door. He told me he could get the honey, and that I was to meet with him there after sunset.

I walked over to the compound after dark, and he described to me what he was about to do. Then he took some newspaper and set it alight. He waved the smoke and flames near to the locker and opened up the door.

He was not exactly a professional beekeeper. He wore no suit and had no equipment. But he knew how to get the honey, and he scooped the honey-combs into a large plastic bucket. I stood by watching. When the raid was over, he presented me with the spoils. He told me to conceal it as best I could because if I didn't, the bees would come for it in the morning. I did my best to extract this dark wild honey and seal it in some jars. The honey-smeared bucket we used was still in the outhouse. Sure enough, the bees came for the honey in the morning, attracted by its scent. Having retrieved what they could, they left. Liz and I enjoyed the honey and knew that this was our newfound friend's way of saying thank you.

Not every story had a happy ending. Michael, the Yoruba driver and mechanic, had a beautiful young daughter just a few years old. But one day she grew sick with a fever and was admitted to a ward. It was polio. Days passed as his little daughter lay there struggling for breath. Paralysis gradually set in. She slept. As she lay there looking so beautiful and peaceful, Michael asked me if it was a good sign. I did not reply. Within a few hours her little life ebbed away, her breathing became shallower and more laboured before she took her final breath and was gone.

We all grieved together and after a short while

Michael said, "*Bring me a blade*." Not long before this took place, I had been reading Chinua Achebe's book, "*Things Fall Apart*". In the story, Achebe describes the life and culture of a powerful Igbo tribe and its leader Okonkwo. As the colonial government introduce new laws, and missionaries introduce a new code of ethics, his world falls apart. The developing new culture strengthens and prevails and Okonkwo, ultimately broken, takes his own life.

I had learned from reading the book that one practice of misinformed tribal people of the time was to mutilate the corpses of little children. Infant mortality was very high, and there was a superstitious belief that an evil spirit sometimes accompanied the birth of a child. This tormenting spirit would take the life of the children one by one. The remedy was to scar the body of the deceased child so that, should the spirit return in any newly born children, the family would recognize it. In this way, the parents hoped to deter the spirit from coming back. Michael intended to mutilate the body of his daughter. I said to Michael, "*It won't come back*". He took my word for it. Soon after, I explained to Michael about the value of having his other children, and any future children he may have, inoculated against polio, measles, tetanus and other contagious diseases. He immediately took my advice.

Nigeria was like that. We were ordinary, well-educated people living amongst a large population, most of whom were poorly educated. Together with our skills, we had much to give. We had the power to change lives for the better because of what we knew or could do. Each constructive intervention, however small, like the flapping of a butterfly's wings, had the power to alter the future for someone for good.

What motivated us to leave the relative comfort and security of living in the U.K.? Why did we choose instead to travel to this wild and often dangerous part of the world? As followers of Christ we had responded literally to our understanding of the mandate to "*Go into all the world and preach the Good News*".[23] We sought to fulfil this calling in several ways. On Sundays, I travelled to church gatherings in the surrounding villages to preach at their services of worship. Bilingual interpreters translated the preaching into the Igala language phrase by phrase. Church services were lively and colourful. The congregation sang harmonies of praise in the Igala language to the rhythm of the beat of clay pot udu drums, each with a hole in the side. These produced a two-tone rhythm when beaten, sometimes with a large pad or a hand and rubber sandal alternately. The men and women were segregated to the right, and the left with an aisle down the middle.

During the worship and the offering, there was always movement in the church to the rhythm of the music. This was not the solemn, sedate event that passes for an offering in the U.K. with a plate handed around to soporific music. A lively, smiling and enthusiastic dancing procession of colourfully dressed congregational worshippers, some with babies strapped to their backs presented offerings. They moved steadily in a line towards the front and back again, all to the rhythm of African song. Sometimes they would stop to take some change out of the offering bucket if they only had a large note at their disposal. They knew how to give cheerfully.

The villagers offered us hospitality, and a cooked meal after the service. Food comprised pounded yam or rice with hot red peppered palm oil stew, generously provided by our hosts. Benefiting as I had from the way I became a Christian brought out the evangelist in me. Why should we keep the good news to ourselves? It was a privilege to preach Christ to these people. This was the best of all gifts we could offer to them. Not only did the Gospel offer fullness of life, it was a message with a promise for the life to come. Being on mission in Africa, there were plenty of opportunities to offer good news to the poor. (There were comparatively few rich people.) We committed to making the most of the opportunities and leave behind a good and lasting legacy.

When Liz and I first stepped out onto Africa's ground together, it was perhaps with an oversimplified, naïve faith, on my part at least. To be told, "*the safest place to be is in the centre of God's will*" has merit. But is there anywhere free from risk or danger? I have learned to expect bad things to happen to good people. Also, good things happen to bad people. This is an imperfect, fallen world. Being

Christians does not exempt us from suffering. Some bad things happened to us while we were in Nigeria. Only by God's grace did we stay the course as long as we did. I have seen the fragile faith of others shipwrecked in the storms of life when things went wrong for them in ways they had not expected. Happily, our troubles, though severe, did not have the power to destroy us.

Experiencing another culture can be enriching. Culture in Nigeria is very different to culture in Scotland. It's not that one culture is better than the other. They are just different. Again, another example from Sunday worship. During the service it was not uncommon for a young man to stretch his arms up in the air, rise slowly from his seat, and go out of the building to urinate at a nearby tree. No one turned a head. Mothers openly breast-fed their babies. Occasionally a curious goat might wander in through the open door. I couldn't help but contrast this to the finesse of drinking tea from china cups after a reflective, ordered church service in the U.K.

Food was not plentiful, so we learned to be resourceful. I planted bananas by the local stream, and grew peanuts, maize, yams, pineapples and tomatoes. Occasionally we bought meat from the local Fulani butcher. He would arrive at random on a bicycle with part of the carcass of a cow or bull, tail dangling down, strapped to the back. We had a paraffin freezer to store the meat.

One day I came up with the idea to buy a whole

live goat to slaughter and butcher. I thought this would keep us going for a while and be the cheaper option. Ejule market was on that day. I travelled to market and returned with the creature in the back of a pickup truck. I tethered the goat inside the out-house.

Following through on my idea wasn't as easy as I thought it might be. However, I went to it armed with a sharp knife intent on doing the deed. Then I had second thoughts. I asked a colleague at the dispensary for some ether. I soaked a cloth with it and laid it over the goat's nose. After a short while, it staggered and at the point of collapse I did the deed.

The problem with reading a book rather than watching TV is that you can't "*look away now*". I had never slaughtered an animal. The blood pumped from the body of the dying animal, forced out by its beating, failing heart. The blood filled nearly half a bucket. I consoled myself with the thought that the animal, anaesthetised as it was by the ether, had been none the wiser. I set to work, gutting, skinning and selecting the parts into meal-sized portions and sealing them in bags to put into the freezer.

While butchering the meat, a young man turned up in distress. He seemed to have become involved in occult practises and was desperate for help. It was not the best time to stop. I had blood all over my hands, and I was eager to clear up and finish before the flies arrived. I asked him to come back in an hour. I never saw him again. Perhaps he was part of a group travelling together and had to leave. Should I have cleaned up, taken a break and given him the time he needed? Perhaps I should. This is just one incident that describes a time when I may have got it wrong. What might have been the butterfly effect for him had I given him the time he needed?

That evening we invited Neil and Jane, both expatriate doctors, over for a goat's meat curry with rice as a special treat. We sat around our primitively constructed table, said grace, and began. But with one mouthful, Jane said, "*Ugh, this tastes like ether*". It was the goat's revenge. The ether had tainted the entire consignment. I don't suppose the leprosy patients minded too much that the meat tasted of ether. We gave it all away to them, and they received it gladly.

I learned something else. I had often read in the Bible about the sacrifices at the temple and the blood of bulls and goats being offered. Taking a knife and slaughtering an animal myself was sobering. It brought home to me the cost, not least to the animal itself. The Old Testament practice of animal sacrifice at temple worship illustrates that forgiveness for wrongdoing can come about only at great cost. It helped to enrich people's understanding in later New Testament times, of Christ's death for us as a sacrifice for sin.

Although it was difficult, eventually Liz and I adapted reasonably well to African culture. It is easy to be critical. But is it really appropriate for us to impose our own Western values on others as though we are better than they are? One quality I witnessed in the culture of African tribes was honour and respect shown by children to parents and younger people to their elders. I never got used to being called "master" by the Africans who worked at the hospital under my supervision. Employing a houseboy to do the chores might appear to be a throwback to colonial times. Africans did not see it that way. For us to refuse to employ a young person meant denying them the opportunity to earn school fees and receive an education.

We had a succession of house helpers. Our favourite was a young boy named Daniel. Daniel was well-mannered and likeable. He was the son of leprosy patients now cured. He was trustworthy. Not everyone was. A favourite trick that some house helpers would practice was to move and hide an item of value to them to see if we noticed. If we said nothing, it might disappear altogether. If we noticed and asked if they had seen it, they would "very helpfully" show us where it was.

Liz and I were now on our second tour and expecting our second child, Alastair. We were glad that David would eventually have a companion and playmate. According to Liz, Alastair's birth was easier than David's. It was not far for us to travel from place to place within the compound; just two hundred yards from our home to the maternity ward. Liz was in labour and got settled into the labour ward bed. There was no ceiling fan, and the room was hot, so I got hold of a standing fan and wired it into the light switch pendant. This brought much-needed relief to Liz, who had been living with her own physical central heating for the latter months of her pregnancy.

Childbirth this time was uncomplicated. Liz wrote in her diary, "*Induction postponed because of C/S. Started 1 p.m. Nothing doing until A.R.M. at 7.30 p.m. Quick labour… male child 9.55 p.m. All well 7Ibs. Praise God.*" So apparently Alastair might have been born earlier that day had it not been that someone at the maternity unit needed a caesarean section.

We travelled back the 200 yds to home later that evening in the pickup truck. The following morning the visitors came, one with a pineapple, another with a live chicken and another with a large bunch of bananas. They wanted to see the white child. "*Well done master*", one of them said to me. Well, Liz didn't know whether to be angry or to laugh. She did all the hard work, and I got the credit. But we knew what our visitor meant. In African culture, if a father has a male first child and then a second male child, he must have done something right.

Two tours in Nigeria of nearly two years each was enough. There were several reasons for this. I had become convinced that it was best for the hospital to employ a capable Nigerian to do the work I was doing. Along with this, I desired to focus my energy more towards greater spiritual input than spend most of my time fixing or building things. For Liz, living and working in this remote and sometimes hostile environment had proved very costly. We knew leaving after only two tours would not go down well with some Christians at home. Some church people appeared to judge those who left the mission field as being failures. Liz, who was finding it increasingly difficult to continue, knew she was between a rock and a hard place. She didn't want to feel as though she was the cause of my leaving the work abroad I had grown to love. She also feared the possibility of frowning disapproval from a few people in our home church when it became apparent that we would not be career missionaries.

David and Alastair's health, wellbeing and education became an increasing cause for concern. We felt strong bonds with our children, and we were not prepared to send them off to boarding school. Not too long after Alastair's birth, we had discovered that he too had the same genetic condition as David. Sacrificing for ourselves is one thing, but we were not prepared to force them into sacrificing for us. I had already been in touch with the Principal of the Scottish Baptist College to explore further future preparation for church ministry at home. Sensing that this phase of ministry in Nigeria was coming to a close, I had already glimpsed what was to be a new beginning for us soon.

Leaving Nigeria was difficult for me. It felt like a bereavement. We could return for a third tour but did not go back. This meant not saying goodbye properly, either to the work or the people. I had recurrent dreams of being back, living and working in

Africa. I would wake up with feelings of disappointment that it had only been a dream. This went on for months and months. Then the dream changed. I dreamt I was in Nigeria at the compound and in my dream, I dreamt that I was not dreaming. These were the cruel symptoms of loss. Many months later my dream changed again. I dreamt I was back in Nigeria and things were not the same. Everything had changed. This was the last dream. The healing had begun.

A generation previously, Dad had left Nigeria and had to transition from living and working abroad to living in the U.K. Now it was my turn to change. My strong advantage was that of having faith in Christ. I could pray and trust God to direct me. My goal was to "*seek first his kingdom*"[24]. The thirty years of Baptist ministry that followed are perhaps the material for another book. We left footprints in Nigeria. Hopefully, these were good and lasting ones.

David and Alastair playing dominoes

◆ ◆ ◆

FOOTPRINTS

FOOTPRINTS

'Footprints – his and mine.
What kinds of footprints am I leaving, in the sands of time?

Christ's footprints shaped the future through the human heart. Saving, changing, healing, ruling, Lord of every part.

What steps will others take because of me?
Who will choose to take the path that follows Thee?

What footprints are we leaving in the lives of others?
On children, parents, husbands, wives; on sisters and on brothers?

What footprints will they leave in turn in whose hearts your word is sown?
Faint footprints that disappear? Or greater steps that others choose to follow in and make their own?

God grant the footprints that I leave will lead to greater things unmeasured though unknown.

(Nigel E. Heath 2012)

Often, significant events in our lives lead to a change of direction. When we change course, this influences others. Dad had a bad day at work. In response, he decided to move on. His decision to do so led directly to the negative consequences for me that I have described here. I had a bad day at home. Embittered, I decided to move on. Consequently, I followed a destructive path that led to negative consequences for others. Some people decided to do some evangelism at a pop festival, and they singled me out. I gave my life to Christ there and then. This altered the course of my life and changed my future from almost certain destruction to a meaningful new life full of promise, purpose and goodness.

At many a crossroad there is a path we would be wise to take, and a turning to avoid. Wisdom appeals to us to choose well. But temptation also seeks to seduce us into following ways that lead to harm. At these turning points we cannot avoid making choices of our own any more than we can escape the daily interaction of human relationships. What is it that determines whether we choose good or bad, right or wrong, wise or unwise? Theologians, philosophers and psychologists alike all debate this subject. I would rather choose the right than debate the mystery. I would rather do what is wise when making daily decisions, whether great or small. Who knows what impact or outcome for good might result from a simple act of kindness or encouragement shown to someone else?

Through life, in all of our experience and learning, each one of us develops a way of seeing and interpreting our world. We develop a "world view". Mine is that of a convinced Christian theist. I attribute the overwhelmingly powerful, potentially life-transforming experience I had at the moment of conversion to there being truth and substance in the historical records of the New Testament. As the Bible puts it, Jesus Christ "*was shown to be the Son of God when he was raised from the dead by the power of the Holy Spirit*"[25]. Inasmuch as this is true (and the proposition appears to withstand a thorough examination of the evidence to support it), then herein lies the explanation for my experience and transformation. I am a believer by choice, based on experience and evidence to back it. I interpret our world from this perspective.

Often, we alter the course and direction of the lives of others, changing their future through the words we speak, the things we do or the choices we make. Others alter the trajectory of our own lives in the same way. Beneath the surface of human exchanges lies a force, a power that Christians identify as the providence of God. As a Christian, I experience conflict at every turning point and crossroads whenever I must make a choice to follow a new direction. I can take the first steps towards doing good, whilst tempted to follow a different path. Looking back over my life, I can see how the benevolent interventions of God assisted me to take the right direction once I had surrendered my stubborn will to Christ.

My call to conversion was like that of a gentle, persuasive whisper spoken by a kind, wise grandparent. God as "grandparent" fully respected my right to say no and hide from me the tears God might otherwise have shed if I had chosen selfishly and refused his invitation. I have learned to recognize that voice. But because it is always a gentle persuasive whisper, not a shout or a command, I still risk getting it wrong. The loud, competing voices of my selfish will can drown out the whispers of God. These seek to seduce me into withholding instead of offering the love I am empowered to give to others.

Missionary service in Nigeria was just the beginning. Liz and I served together in pastoral ministry for ten years in Edinburgh and over twenty years in East Kilbride. This provided us with an opportunity to be at the very heart and centre of groups of Christian people, themselves committed to the cause we shared. I have no regrets. Every word and deed for good had the potential to alter the direction of other people's lives, leading to better outcomes. We continue to serve today.

I know that at 67 years of age I have started

on the home run. As nature would have it, my body, already experiencing the signs of ageing, will eventually fail. Faith informs my hope and expectation that, as surely as Christ died for me and was raised from death, I too have a future when my spirit passes from this frail and mortal frame into the presence of God. I am grateful for health of body and mind and the potential of years remaining in which to be productive.

I can yet leave footprints in the lives of others. I can continue to make wise choices. I can make the most of the opportunities to do good and right. More than anything else, I want my life to be of lasting worth. In two or three generations time, the living will not remember me. On leaning tombstones covered with moss and lichen in abandoned churchyards, we read the names of people who were once the stewards of life. They were the tenants of our world during their lifetime, but they have long vacated. They lived and breathed and ate and drank. They laughed and cried. They married and had children of their own. They inhabited this thin biosphere of life for a season. They lived and died. They made their choices, leaving footprints of their own. Few will be remembered. Those whose names are notable, often have left some of the deepest, largest footprints. Those with the most power had the best opportunity to change the world for the better. We remember famous people like Gandhi or Hitler, who impacted our world contrastingly for good and ill. But others whose names are not remembered made their impact too. There are people who, though their names, lives and stories were not recorded, have by their lives have affected generations to come. Though their names have been forgotten, the impact of their lives remains and continues on.

While on holiday in the north of Scotland I was walking along the coast near to Findochty overlooking the Moray Firth in Banffshire. I came across a small bridge, erected in memory of "Joe". Joe meant so much to his devoted friends that they wanted to commemorate his life. I journaled:

"Why is it that moments of melancholy and thoughts of the brevity of life stimulate the centres of creativity? Am I alone in this? In the stillness of a winter's morning, with the sun shining brightly over Findochty harbour viewed from my window, reflecting on a conversation I had with someone the day before, alone in the silence before the activities of the day I reflect once more on life's brevity.

Yesterday we crossed a bridge on a golf course, built in memory to 'Joe' so the plaque read; in memory to his name, friendship and character. I did not know Joe, but Joe's friends loved him and remembered him with fondness enough to erect a small bridge on a golf course in his memory. Joe has gone; yet his friends had glimpsed the value of a human life and sought to preserve his memory. For this, passers-by remember them too. But passers-by in years to come will not remember

Joe, and as the salt sea air continues to corrode the steel to rust and flakes away the paint already disappearing from the plaque, and as the mortar crumbles between the stone block construction of the bridge, will anyone think it worthwhile to repair this monument and keep his memory alive for passers-by to notice and reflect upon for the years to come?

We are a footprint in time; a candle that burns long and slow. We are as a coin in a meter with the clock ticking down. We are, as the scripture says, 'a mist that appears for a little while and then is gone', a flower of the field that buds and blossoms before withering and perishing. Life here is brief. Life eternal is unending — a breaking through into the dawning of a new dimension within God's eternal presence as our mortal body crumbles before powers of nature and our temporal life comes to a close.

Life is not so 'meaningless' as the writer of Ecclesiastes imagined it to be — not to those who have discovered life's true meaning and unending hope. May those who have the light of life allow that light to burn brightly for this brief time we are here on earth and brighten the day for others with their presence. Opportunities evaporate as quickly as the morning dew that glistens on the blades of grass at dawn, disappearing as the sun rises in its strength.

Let the footprint on life that you leave be firm and large and lasting. Others may forget your name, but your footprint will always remain in the lives of others for generations to come. Make it good. Make it lasting."

Few people have heard of the school librarian Blanche Caffiere. This lady once noticed a nerdy, skinny young boy with dysgraphia whose handwriting was atrocious, and whose desk was very untidy. She also noted his love for reading. She decided to encourage him and nurture his interest, guiding him to books she knew he would like. That boy was Bill Gates, entrepreneur and founder of Microsoft. Bill Gates went on in life to contribute immensely to global learning and communication. Out of his billions, he and his wife Melinda set up a philanthropic foundation. They set aside $1 billion from this to fight malaria. That's a big footprint. Was there a pivotal moment in Bill Gates life that caused him to choose to help people live and not die by providing this service? Bill Gates wrote, *"I often trace the beginning of our foundation to an article about children in poor countries dying from diseases eliminated long ago in the U.S. But I should give some credit as well to the dedicated librarian and teacher who helped me find my strengths when I was nine years old."* [26]

I found a coin in a car park. I picked it up and kept it, and I let my imagination run. What difference did that coin make? It got me writing. The rest of your life and mine is ahead of us, and you will leave your footprint too. I hope that through reading my story, you will find something here that will help you make good, wise and courageous choices in response to life's often challenging events. Your life is a pen that, every day, writes the new page of a story others will read as history. May the choices you make transform an otherwise future deficit for you and for others into a superabundance for generations to come.

AUTUMN TURNS TO WINTER

The rich foliage of autumn's morn appears.

The darkness of the night has cloaked the winter's chilling kiss.
The signs of ageing and of change herald the season of my fears.
Too soon are gone the summer days of warmth and light I miss.

A blanket tapestry of browns of greens of orange leaves and red;
The beauty of the trees adorned in glory,
Betray those who gaze in wonder into being misled.
Winter's final kiss of death will tell a different story.

Why is life's autumn season with such beauty dressed?
Why save such glory to adorn us at the ending of our days?
Tis nature's crown that celebrates our fruitfulness;
Tis life's farewell before the parting of our ways.

(Nigel E. Heath – 10th September 2012)

"whoever saves a life,
it is considered as if he saved an entire world."[27]

[1]East Midlands colloquial greeting

[2] Welsh for "good morning"

[3] East Midlands "give me a bit"

[4] Welsh for "please"

[5] Cannabis resin

[6] Cannabis resin sprinkled into tobacco in a long roll-up cigarette

[7] Purchase

[8] "Speed" - amphetamines, "mandies"- Mandrax, "dropping acid" - taking LSD, "s**t" - cannabis resin. "Joints" and "spliffs" large roll-up cigarettes laced with cannabis. "Horse" - heroin.

[9] £1's worth of cannabis

[10] A weighed ounce

[11] False

[12] "bloodclaat" means menstrual garment

[13] Titus 1:15

[14] Revelation 3:20

[15] John 3:3

[16] Matthew 18:3

[17] John 4:35

[18] Proverbs 28:10

[19] Job 2:12

[20] Judges chapter 6

[21] Joshua 1:4 (King James Bible)

[22] "Worldwide Evangelisation Crusade" - Later named "WEC International

[23] Mark 16:15

[24] Matthew 6:33

[25] Romans 1:4 (New Living Translation)

[26] https://www.gatesnotes.com/Education/A-Teacher-Who-Changed-My-Life (accessed 6th August 2019)

[27] Jerusalem Talmud, Sanhedrin 4:1 (22a)

Printed in Great Britain
by Amazon